# Prentice Hall

# LITERATURE
## *Timeless Voices, Timele*

D1466394

## Bronze Level

# Performance Assessment and Portfolio Management

Prentice Hall

Upper Saddle River, New Jersey
Glenview, Illinois
Needham, Massachusetts

ISBN 0-13-062392-X

3 4 5 6 7 8 9 10    06 05 04 03 02

# Contents

# Portfolio Management

# Portfolio Management

## Portfolios in Your Classroom

If the classroom is a place where real and engaging work goes on, a portfolio is a device for collecting and honoring writing samples that show this work. Through the portfolio, student effort can be dignified and celebrated in a public forum that parents, students, community members, and administrators may understand and participate in. Portfolios offer the teacher and the student a reasonable way to look at real accomplishments in writing and a reliable way to assess those accomplishments. However, portfolio use comes with a price tag: It costs time and it costs effort.

## Contents: Decide by Collaboration

What could a portfolio contain? This question can spark a good discussion for the teacher and the class at the beginning of the year. A group of teachers may want to address this topic as an initial staff discussion. What do we want our students to know or be able to do? Evidence of these knowings and doings should be found in the portfolio.

## Design: Guidance and Choice

Teachers must be ready to give steady guidance to reluctant or inexperienced students, mentoring to others, and support to risk-takers and "gifted" writers. Using *Prentice Hall Literature,* a teacher might stress one writing mode each month or each quarter. Here is a sample plan for a middle school grade on traditional calendar year:

**September:** Letters, business and friendly. (Write to your summer buddy and tell how school looks so far. Write to a product manufacturer supporting or criticizing quality, packaging, advertising.)

**November:** Interviews (Interview an older family member about family holiday customs. Interview school staff members about changes in school since the "old days.")

**January:** Narratives (Brainstorm moments of personal or group experience, or create a story line of partial or complete fiction, to be published in a class literary magazine.)

**March:** Essays (Take a stand on some current or historical issue. Write an opinion paper for a newspaper or periodical, or a debating speech to present to the class.)

**May:** Poetry (Collect favorite poems and write some of your own in a similar or contrasting style. Send your poetic impressions of school, spring, current events, or friends to appropriate individuals.)

The teacher of younger students may want to include language play activities in such a schedule. The teacher of older students may want to emphasize the essay and business documents, modeling, and works of increasing complexity.

The teacher of any grade level might arrange lessons around each writing mode. The *Prentice Hall Literature* anthologies present models of classic, engaging works in various modes. The Writing Workshops within each unit provide strategies and guidelines for creating each type of writing. The teacher could ask students to focus on the writing mode for a particular time period and produce at least one finished piece by a certain deadline. During March and April, for example, formal instruction could focus on the essay form; essays of all kinds, available in students' textbooks or elsewhere in the classroom, could be read aloud. Others could be featured in the library. Within that period, students might produce several essays or work independently on other forms of writing. An author's circle could occur each week, with the more proficient and confident students reading their essays aloud, and others reacting to and learning from them.

## Management: Checklists and Observation

What kind of management challenges does this process present? Keeping track of what students are working on is less complicated with a checklist that teacher or students fill out regularly. Periodic observation and interviews with students will help the teacher track their growth, level of engagement, and range of writing experiences. As students work and talk about their work, the teacher can assess the program of lessons needed for the group and for individuals: What writing skills, writing modes, or craft instruction does the class especially need? What reinforcements do individuals or small groups need? Quarterly reviews of the portfolio collection by students and teachers, with students doing the bulk of the record keeping, will help keep the process manageable and provide the reflective factor students need to become "owners" of the collection.

Can one portfolio serve more than one master? School districts and states may apply different standards to the contents of a portfolio. However, after meeting imposed requirements, the teacher and students might decide for themselves what kind of portfolio they want included in their class collection. They may elect to use "growth" or "development" portfolios with samples of each student's earliest to most recent writings in it. Or they may prefer "showcase" portfolios that include only each student's "best pieces." In some places, where there are specified contents for statewide assessment, classes create a large folder with developmental pieces in it and a pull-out section for official assessment.

## Topics: Chosen or Imposed?

Experienced teachers know that students will work harder on projects they help design. Are there valid reasons for mixing elective and assigned pieces in a portfolio? If teachers (or districts or states) want to see how students operate under regulated conditions, they might ask from time to time that everyone write to a single prompt. There might also be writing modes on the teacher's agenda that a student chooses never to address (*e.g.*, a student may never elect to write a business letter). The teacher may feel the need to collect this kind of sample with an imposed prompt.

## Portfolio Diversity: Folder or Steamer Trunk?

Should there be a record of samples other than writing? For example, should there be audiotapes, videotapes, or disks? Teachers are getting increasingly creative with these media. Should there be notations on reading experiences, artwork, research, or presentations?

Some schools are buying blank tapes or disks for each student. Recordings of dramatic readings and other oral language performances then go into the folder with the student's written work. Such additions serve to enrich the record of student experience.

## Curriculum Outline

What kind of curriculum outline would help to support ongoing portfolio collections and review? Should a school teach different topics and writing modes across grades 6–12? This is a particularly important question if we want portfolio collections to reflect the rich and broad range of experiences of diverse students taught by diverse teachers. Some literature units and activities invite responses in particular writing modes; unexpected contemporary issues and events will affect some student populations and not others. An open and collegial staff atmosphere might allow teachers to assure each other that they will furnish students with certain writing opportunities at certain times.

## Criteria: Back to Collaboration

How will teachers assess portfolios? Before individuals or groups begin to assess a portfolio of student writing, they must decide which aspects of writing they value. Another discussion could be productive here. Parents, teachers, and students could answer together the question "What are the qualities (criteria) of good writing?" The group will probably list organization, clarity, style, mechanics, and perhaps a few other features. Those making the decisions must take pains to be specific in defining the criteria they choose to judge by. If the group operates from an already established list, the group should take even more time to understand and accept that list. Many schools have adopted the "official" criteria (purpose, organization, details, voice, and mechanics) for their own use in classroom record keeping and reporting as well as the official statewide assessment. In *Prentice Hall Literature* (and also in this booklet) rubrics are provided for assessing each mode of writing.

How should we describe the different levels students are achieving in order to assess individual work and growth? Again, teachers can generate their own descriptions of good, fair, and poor achievement. Or they can use the rubrics provided with this program.

## Ultimate Goal: Student Reflection

Portfolios are useful as evidence of achievement and of growth. But to fulfill its maximum potential, the portfolio must move the student to critical thinking, analysis, and reflection as he or she chooses what to include in the portfolio. Each year, or even better, each quarter, a teacher might ask the student to choose a "best piece" of writing from the portfolio and to articulate reasons for the choice. A student involved in good classroom instruction and support will make intelligent choices, showing the kind of learning and analytical skills we want for all our students. At the end of the year, the student can be asked to select a range of "best pieces" that demonstrate good letter writing, creative writing, persuasive writing, and critical thinking. With hard work, patience, and luck, we can send our students on with a portfolio reflecting who and what they are, and we can help them feel proud of the good things they do.

# Suggested Organization and Inspiration Tools

## Organization Tools

1. Grid for teaching week to show status of current student projects

2. Box to keep portfolios in

3. Rack for folders of work-in-progress

4. Computers or word processors

5. 3-hole binder notebook with tabs marking sections for each student (to use for random teacher observations, samples, conference notes)

6. Benchmark collections: samples of writing illustrating strength in each criterion you value. Some samples are included in this booklet. You may wish to collect others to share with your students.

7. Timeline for topics and writing modes you will emphasize throughout the year

## Inspiration Tools

1. Bank of audiences and purposes for writing

2. Names of recipients for letters or subjects of interviews

3. Connections to local media for publication, collaboration, and public relations purposes

4. Access to the Internet

5. Authentic, engaging topics for student research

6. Rigorous and engaging professional development for teachers that begins with a comprehensive look at their own literacy

7. Establishment of support networks among parent populations

# Performance Assessment: Rubrics

# Rubrics for Narration: Autobiographical Narrative

*Use one or both of the following sets of criteria to evaluate autobiographical narratives.*

| Criteria | Not very | Rating Scale | | | Very |
|---|---|---|---|---|---|
| How well does the story focus on the central conflict? | 1 | 2 | 3 | 4 | 5 |
| How well does it stick to first-person point of view? | 1 | 2 | 3 | 4 | 5 |
| How well sequenced are the events? | 1 | 2 | 3 | 4 | 5 |
| How well do details and dialogue portray the people, setting, and actions? | 1 | 2 | 3 | 4 | 5 |
| How well do details convey thoughts and feelings? | 1 | 2 | 3 | 4 | 5 |
| How well does the writer use precise nouns and verbs? | 1 | 2 | 3 | 4 | 5 |

| | Score 4 | Score 3 | Score 2 | Score 1 |
|---|---|---|---|---|
| Audience and Purpose | Contains an engaging introduction; successfully entertains or presents a theme | Contains a somewhat engaging introduction; entertains or presents a theme | Contains an introduction; attempts to entertain or to present a theme | Begins abruptly or confusingly; leaves purpose unclear |
| Organization | Creates an interesting, clear narrative; told from a consistent point of view | Presents a clear sequence of events; told from a specific point of view | Presents a mostly clear sequence of events; contains inconsistent points of view | Presents events without logical order; lacks a consistent point of view |
| Elaboration | Provides insight into character; develops plot; contains dialogue | Contains details and dialogue that develop character and plot | Contains details that develop plot; contains some dialogue | Contains few or no details to develop characters or plot |
| Use of Language | Uses word choice and tone to reveal story's theme; contains no errors in grammar, punctuation, or spelling | Uses interesting and fresh word choices; contains few errors in grammar, punctuation, and spelling | Uses some clichés and trite expressions; contains some errors in grammar, punctuation, and spelling | Uses uninspired word choices; has many errors in grammar, punctuation, and spelling |

# Rubrics for Description: Descriptive Composition

*Use one or both of the following sets of criteria to evaluate descriptive compositions.*

| Criteria | Rating Scale | | | | |
|---|---|---|---|---|---|
| | **Not very** | | | | **Very** |
| How well are sensory details used? | 1 | 2 | 3 | 4 | 5 |
| How well is a main impression made? | 1 | 2 | 3 | 4 | 5 |
| How clear and consistent is the organization? | 1 | 2 | 3 | 4 | 5 |
| How well is descriptive language used? | 1 | 2 | 3 | 4 | 5 |

| | Score 4 | Score 3 | Score 2 | Score 1 |
|---|---|---|---|---|
| Audience and Purpose | Creates a memorable main impression through effective use of details | Creates a main impression through use of details | Contains details that distract from main impression | Contains details that are unfocused and create no main impression |
| Organization | Is organized consistently, logically, and effectively | Is organized consistently | Is organized, but not consistently | Is disorganized and confusing |
| Elaboration | Contains rich sensory language that appeals to the five senses | Contains some rich sensory language | Contains some rich sensory language, but it appeals to only one or two of the senses | Contains only flat language |
| Use of Language | Uses vivid and precise adjectives; contains no errors in grammar, punctuation, or spelling | Uses some vivid and precise adjectives; contains few errors in grammar, punctuation, and spelling | Uses few vivid and precise adjectives; contains some errors in grammar, punctuation, and spelling | Uses no vivid adjectives; contains many errors in grammar, punctuation, and spelling |

# Rubrics for Expository Writing: Problem-Solution Composition

*Use one or both of the following sets of criteria to evaluate problem-solution compositions.*

| Criteria | Not very | Rating Scale | | Very |
|---|---|---|---|---|
| How clearly stated is the problem? | 1 2 | 3 | 4 | 5 |
| How well presented are the solutions? | 1 2 | 3 | 4 | 5 |
| How strong and convincing is the support? | 1 2 | 3 | 4 | 5 |
| How well are possible objections addressed? | 1 2 | 3 | 4 | 5 |
| How varied are the sentences? | 1 2 | 3 | 4 | 5 |

| | Score 4 | Score 3 | Score 2 | Score 1 |
|---|---|---|---|---|
| **Audience and Purpose** | Coherently states and explains the problem; uses strong and convincing language that is appropriate to the intended audience | States and describes the problem; uses convincing language that is appropriate to the intended audience | States and briefly describes the problem; uses unconvincing language that is mostly appropriate to the intended audience | Fails to state the problem and explains it vaguely; uses unconvincing language that is somewhat appropriate to the intended audience |
| **Organization** | Demonstrates the relationship between the problem and its possible solutions; maintains anl appropriate organizational structure | Addresses the relationship between the problem and its possible solutions; maintains an appropriate organizational structure | Alludes to the relationship between the problem and its possible solutions; uses a somewhat appropriate organizational structure | Fails to relate the problem to its possible solutions; does not use an apparent organizational structure |
| **Elaboration** | Convincingly supports several possible solutions; thoroughly addresses possible objections | Strongly supports one or more possible solutions; adequately addresses possible objections | Supports one or more possible solutions; attempts to address possible objections | Mentions one possible solution, but fails to support it; addresses no possible objections |
| **Use of Language** | Effectively varies sentences; discusses the problem and its possible solutions with strong and compelling words | Varies sentences; discusses the problem and its possible solutions with strong and somewhat compelling words | Varies sentences somewhat; discusses the problem and its possible solutions with some vague or purposeless words | Fails to vary sentences; discusses the problem and its possible solutions with mostly vague or purposeless words |

# Rubrics for Persuasion: Persuasive Composition

*Use one or both of the following sets of criteria to evaluate persuasive compositions.*

| Criteria | Rating Scale | | | | |
|---|---|---|---|---|---|
| | Not very | | | | Very |
| How evident is it that the issue has more than one "side"? | 1 | 2 | 3 | 4 | 5 |
| How clearly is the position stated? | 1 | 2 | 3 | 4 | 5 |
| How well is the evidence organized? | 1 | 2 | 3 | 4 | 5 |
| How clearly is the evidence presented? | 1 | 2 | 3 | 4 | 5 |

| | Score 4 | Score 3 | Score 2 | Score 1 |
|---|---|---|---|---|
| **Audience and Purpose** | Provides arguments, illustrations, and words that forcefully appeal to the audience and effectively serve persuasive purpose | Provides arguments, illustrations, and words that appeal to the audience and serve the persuasive purpose | Provides some support that appeals to the audience and serves the persuasive purpose | Shows little attention to the audience or persuasive purpose |
| **Organization** | Uses clear, consistent organizational strategy | Uses clear organizational strategy with occasional inconsistencies | Uses inconsistent organizational strategy | Shows lack of organizational strategy; writing is confusing |
| **Elaboration** | Provides specific, well-elaborated support for the writer's position | Provides some elaborated support for the writer's position | Provides some support, but with little elaboration | Lacks support |
| **Use of Language** | Uses transitions to connect ideas smoothly; shows few mechanical errors | Uses some transitions; shows few mechanical errors | Uses few transitions; shows some mechanical errors | Shows little connection between ideas; shows many mechanical errors |

# Rubrics for Exposition: Summary

*Use one or both of the following sets of criteria to evaluate summaries.*

| Criteria | Rating Scale | | | | |
| --- | --- | --- | --- | --- | --- |
| | Not very | | | | Very |
| How clear is the statement of the main idea? | 1 | 2 | 3 | 4 | 5 |
| How significant are the details? | 1 | 2 | 3 | 4 | 5 |
| How well does the summary reflect the deeper meaning of the work? | 1 | 2 | 3 | 4 | 5 |
| How brief and precise is the writing? | 1 | 2 | 3 | 4 | 5 |
| How effective are the transitions? | 1 | 2 | 3 | 4 | 5 |

| | Score 4 | Score 3 | Score 2 | Score 1 |
| --- | --- | --- | --- | --- |
| Audience and Purpose | Clearly and effectively projects the deeper meaning of the work being summarized; reflects the writer's own understanding | Projects a grasp of the deeper meaning of the work being summarized; reflects the writer's own understanding | Projects a sense of the deeper meaning of the work being summarized; indicates the writer's own understanding | Projects little awareness of the deeper meaning of the work being summarized; indicates a lack of the writer's own understanding |
| Organization | Clearly states the main idea; includes the most significant details | States the main idea; includes important details, but some may not be significant | Indicates the main idea somewhat vaguely; includes important details, but some may not be significant | Fails to include the main idea; includes some details, but most are insignificant |
| Elaboration | Includes only the essential details and explains their significance and relevance to the main idea | Includes mostly essential details and explains their significance and relevance to the main idea somewhat | Includes some inessential details and vaguely explains their significance and relevance to the main idea | Includes random details that may or may not be significant and fails to explain their relevance to the main idea |
| Use of Language | Effectively connects ideas with transitions; uses language that is brief and concise | Connect ideas with transitions; uses language that is mostly brief and concise | Uses some transitions to connect ideas; uses language that is not as brief and concise as prescribed by a summary format | Uses few, if any, transitions to connect ideas; uses language that is not brief and concise |

# Rubrics for Narration: Short Story

*Use one or both of the following sets of criteria to evaluate short stories.*

| Criteria | Rating Scale | | | | |
|---|---|---|---|---|---|
| | Not very | | | | Very |
| How well are the characters developed? | 1 | 2 | 3 | 4 | 5 |
| How well is the setting described? | 1 | 2 | 3 | 4 | 5 |
| How suspenseful is the plot? | 1 | 2 | 3 | 4 | 5 |
| How consistent are the tense and point of view? | 1 | 2 | 3 | 4 | 5 |
| How well are meaningful actions described? | 1 | 2 | 3 | 4 | 5 |
| How well does the story *show* rather than *tell*? | 1 | 2 | 3 | 4 | 5 |

| | Score 4 | Score 3 | Score 2 | Score 1 |
|---|---|---|---|---|
| Audience and Purpose | Contains an engaging introduction; successfully entertains or presents a theme | Contains a somewhat engaging introduction; entertains or presents a theme | Contains an introduction; attempts to entertain or to present a theme | Begins abruptly or confusingly; leaves purpose unclear |
| Organizatio | Creates an interesting, clear narrative; told from a consistent point of view | Presents a clear sequence of events; told from a specific point of view | Presents a mostly clear sequence of events; contains inconsistent points of view | Presents events without logical order; lacks a consistent point of view |
| Elaboration | Provides insight into character; develops plot; contains dialogue | Contains details and dialogue that develop character and plot | Contains details that develop plot; contains some dialogue | Contains few or no details to develop characters or plot |
| Use of Language | Uses word choice and tone to reveal story's theme; contains no errors in grammar, punctuation, or spelling | Uses interesting and fresh word choices; contains few errors in grammar, punctuation, and spelling | Uses some clichés and trite expressions; contains some errors in grammar, punctuation, and spelling | Uses uninspired word choices; has many errors in grammar, punctuation, and spelling |

# Rubrics for Research: Research Report

*Use one or both of the following sets of criteria to evaluate research reports.*

| Criteria | Rating Scale Not very | | | | Very |
|---|---|---|---|---|---|
| How clear is the overall focus or main idea? | 1 | 2 | 3 | 4 | 5 |
| How well is the information gathered from a variety of sources? | 1 | 2 | 3 | 4 | 5 |
| How clearly organized is the report? | 1 | 2 | 3 | 4 | 5 |
| How well is each point supported by credible facts and details? | 1 | 2 | 3 | 4 | 5 |
| How well does the report combine quoted and paraphrased information? | 1 | 2 | 3 | 4 | 5 |
| How clear and accurate are the citations and bibliography? | 1 | 2 | 3 | 4 | 5 |

| | Score 4 | Score 3 | Score 2 | Score 1 |
|---|---|---|---|---|
| Audience and Purpose | Focuses on a clearly-stated thesis, starting from a well-framed question; gives complete citations | Focuses on a clearly stated thesis; gives citations | Focuses mainly on the chosen topic; gives some citations | Presents information without a clear focus; few or no citations |
| Organizatio | Presents information in logical order, emphasizing details of central importance | Presents information in logical order | Presents information logically, but organization is poor in places | Presents information in a scattered, disorganized manner |
| Elaboration | Draws clear conclusions from information gathered from multiple sources | Draws conclusions from information gathered from multiple sources | Explains and interprets some information | Presents information with little or no interpretation or synthesis |
| Use of Language | Shows overall clarity and fluency; contains few mechanical errors | Shows good sentence variety; contains some errors in spelling, punctuation, or usage | Uses awkward or overly simple sentence structures; contains many mechanical errors | Contains incomplete thoughts and mechanical errors that make the writing confusing |

# Rubrics for Response to Literature

*Use one or both of the following sets of criteria to evaluate responses to literature.*

| Criteria | Rating Scale Not very — Very | | | | |
|---|---|---|---|---|---|
| How well is the response based on a strong, interesting judgment of some aspect of the literary work? | 1 | 2 | 3 | 4 | 5 |
| How well does the interpretation reflect careful reading, understanding, and insight? | 1 | 2 | 3 | 4 | 5 |
| How clearly is the response organized around several ideas, premises, or images? | 1 | 2 | 3 | 4 | 5 |
| How adequate are the supporting examples and textual evidence? | 1 | 2 | 3 | 4 | 5 |
| How effectively does the writer refer to literary elements to express the response? | 1 | 2 | 3 | 4 | 5 |

| | Score 4 | Score 3 | Score 2 | Score 1 |
|---|---|---|---|---|
| Audience and Purpose | Presents sufficient background on the work(s); presents the writer's reactions forcefully | Presents background on the work(s); presents the writer's reactions clearly | Presents some background on the work(s); presents the writer's reactions at points | Presents little or no background on the work(s); presents few of the writer's reactions |
| Organization | Presents points in logical order, smoothly connecting them to the overall focus | Presents points in logical order and connects many to the overall focus | Organizes points poorly in places; connects some points to an overall focus | Presents information in a scattered, disorganized manner |
| Elaboration | Supports reactions and evaluations with elaborated reasons and well-chosen examples | Supports reactions and evaluations with specific reasons and examples | Supports some reactions and evaluations with reasons and examples | Offers little support for reactions and evaluations |
| Use of Language | Shows overall clarity and fluency; uses precise, evaluative words; makes few mechanical errors | Shows good sentence variety; uses some precise evaluative terms; makes some mechanical errors | Uses awkward or overly simple sentence structures and vague evaluative terms; makes many mechanical errors | Presents incomplete thoughts; makes mechanical errors that create confusion |

# Rubrics for Exposition: Comparison-and-Contrast Essay

*Use one or both of the following sets of criteria to evaluate comparison-and-contrast essays.*

| Criteria | Rating Scale | | | | |
|---|---|---|---|---|---|
| | Not very | | | | Very |
| How clearly does the essay involve two or more related subjects? | 1 | 2 | 3 | 4 | 5 |
| How well do the supporting details show both similarities and differences? | 1 | 2 | 3 | 4 | 5 |
| How clear, consistent and appropriate is the method of organization? | 1 | 2 | 3 | 4 | 5 |
| How well balanced is the support of both (or all) subjects? | 1 | 2 | 3 | 4 | 5 |
| How smooth are the transitions between paragraphs? | 1 | 2 | 3 | 4 | 5 |

| | Score 4 | Score 3 | Score 2 | Score 1 |
|---|---|---|---|---|
| Audience and Purpose | Clearly attracts audience interest in the comparison-contrast analysis | Adequately attracts audience interest in the comparison-contrast analysis | Provides a reason for the comparison-contrast analysis | Does not provide a reason for a comparison-contrast analysis |
| Organization | Clearly presents information in a consistent organization best suited to the topic | Presents information using an organization suited to the topic | Chooses an organization not suited to comparison and contrast | Shows a lack of organizational strategy |
| Elaboration | Elaborates ideas with facts, details, or examples; uses all information for comparison and contrast | Elaborates most ideas with facts, details, or examples; uses most information for comparison and contrast | Does not elaborate all ideas; does not use enough details for comparison and contrast | Does not provide facts or examples to support a comparison and contrast |
| Use of Language | Demonstrates excellent sentence and vocabulary variety; includes very few mechanical errors | Demonstrates adequate sentence and vocabulary variety; includes few mechanical errors | Demonstrates repetitive use of sentence structure and vocabulary; includes many mechanical errors | Demonstrates poor use of language; generates confusion; includes many mechanical errors |

# Rubrics for Multimedia Report

*Use one or both of the following sets of criteria to evaluate multimedia reports.*

| Criteria | Rating Scale | | | | |
|---|---|---|---|---|---|
| | Not very | | | | Very |
| How well does the report focus on one clear topic? | 1 | 2 | 3 | 4 | 5 |
| How clear and consistent is the bibliography? | 1 | 2 | 3 | 4 | 5 |
| How appropriate is the word-processing format? | 1 | 2 | 3 | 4 | 5 |
| How well does the database or spreadsheet express and manage information? | 1 | 2 | 3 | 4 | 5 |
| How strong and dramatic is the visual component? | 1 | 2 | 3 | 4 | 5 |
| How strong and dramatic is the audio component? | 1 | 2 | 3 | 4 | 5 |

| | Score 4 | Score 3 | Score 2 | Score 1 |
|---|---|---|---|---|
| Audience and Purpose | Successfully focuses on one clear topic; effectively applies visual and audio components | Focuses on one clear topic; appropriately applies visual and audio components | Focuses on one topic; applies visual and audio components somewhat inappropriately | Fails to focus on one topic; applies visual and audio components inappropriately |
| Organization | Uses an appropriate word-processing format; makes use of database or spreadsheet formats to advantageously organize information | Uses a somewhat appropriate word-processing format; makes use of database or spreadsheet formats to organize information | Uses a somewhat inappropriate word-processing format; attempts to use database or spreadsheet formats to organize information | Uses an inappropriate word-processing format; does not use database or spreadsheet formats to organize information |
| Elaboration | Includes a clear and consistent bibliography; uses visual and audio components to elaborate on and enhance written material | Includes a consistent bibliography; uses visual and audio components to elaborate on written material | Includes a somewhat inconsistent bibliography; uses visual and audio components with a vague connection to written material | Includes an inconsistent bibliography; uses visual and audio components with little, if any, connection to written material |
| Use of Language | Chooses words that precisely address the topic; effectively uses language to integrate different types of media | Chooses words that adequately address the topic; uses language to integrate different types of media | Chooses words that address the topic; attempts to use language to integrate different types of media | Chooses words that inadequately address the topic; fails to use language to integrate different types of media |

# Rubrics for Exposition: Cause-and-Effect Essay

*Use one or both of the following sets of criteria to evaluate cause-and-effect essays.*

| Criteria | Not very | | | | |
|---|---|---|---|---|---|
| How well are causes and effects linked? | 1 | 2 | 3 | 4 | 5 |
| How clear is the relationship between a cause and an effect? | 1 | 2 | 3 | 4 | 5 |
| How consistent and appropriate is the organization? | 1 | 2 | 3 | 4 | 5 |
| How well established is the purpose of demonstrating a relationship between causes and effects? | 1 | 2 | 3 | 4 | 5 |

| | Score 4 | Score 3 | Score 2 | Score 1 |
|---|---|---|---|---|
| Audience and Purpose | Consistently targets an audience through word choice and details; clearly identifies purpose in thesis statement | Targets an audience through most word choice and details; identifies purpose in thesis statement | Misses a target audience by including a wide range of word choice and details; presents no clear purpose | Addresses no specific audience or purpose |
| Organization | Presents a clear, consistent organizational strategy to show cause and effect | Presents a clear organizational strategy with occasional inconsistencies; shows cause and effect | Presents an inconsistent organizational strategy; creates illogical presentation of causes and effects | Demonstrates a lack of organizational strategy; creates a confusing presentation |
| Elaboration | Successfully links causes with effects; fully elaborates connections among ideas | Links causes with effects; elaborates connections among most ideas | Links some causes with some effects; elaborates connections among most ideas | Develops and elaborates no links between causes and effects |
| Use of Language | Chooses clear transitions to convey ideas; presents very few mechanical errors | Chooses transitions to convey ideas; presents few mechanical errors | Misses some opportunities for transitions to convey ideas; presents many mechanical errors | Demonstrates poor use of language; presents many mechanical errors |

# Rubrics for Exposition: Explanation of a Process

*Use one or both of the following sets of criteria to evaluate process explanations.*

| Criteria | Not very | | Rating Scale | | Very |
|---|---|---|---|---|---|
| How focused is the explanation on an appropriate topic? | 1 | 2 | 3 | 4 | 5 |
| How clearly defined are terms that may be new to readers? | 1 | 2 | 3 | 4 | 5 |
| How well organized are the steps in the process? | 1 | 2 | 3 | 4 | 5 |
| How well do visual aids enhance the explanation of procedures? | 1 | 2 | 3 | 4 | 5 |
| How well do organization and formatting aid comprehension? | 1 | 2 | 3 | 4 | 5 |

| | Score 4 | Score 3 | Score 2 | Score 1 |
|---|---|---|---|---|
| Audience and Purpose | Clearly focuses on procedures leading to a well-defined end | Focuses on procedures leading to a well-defined end | Includes procedures related to an end, but presents some vaguely | Includes only vague descriptions of procedures and results |
| Organization | Gives instructions in logical order; subdivides complex actions into steps | Gives instructions in logical order; subdivides some complex actions into steps | For the most part, gives instructions in logical order | Gives instructions in a scattered, disorganized manner |
| Elaboration | Provides appropriate amount of detail; gives needed explanations | Provides appropriate amount of detail; gives some explanations | Provides some detail; gives few explanations | Provides few details; gives few or no explanations |
| Use of Language | Shows overall clarity and fluency; uses transitions effectively; contains few mechanical errors | Shows some sentence variety; uses some transitions; includes few mechanical errors | Uses awkward or overly simple sentence structures; contains many mechanical errors | Contains incomplete thoughts and confusing mechanical errors |

# Rubrics for Writing for Assessment

*Use one or both of the following sets of criteria to evaluate writing for assessment.*

| Criteria | Not very | Rating Scale | | | Very |
|---|---|---|---|---|---|
| How well does the thesis address the writing prompt? | 1 | 2 | 3 | 4 | 5 |
| How well do the main ideas and supporting details support the thesis? | 1 | 2 | 3 | 4 | 5 |
| How well elaborated is each idea that is presented? | 1 | 2 | 3 | 4 | 5 |
| How appropriate are the details? | 1 | 2 | 3 | 4 | 5 |
| How clear and consistent is the organization? | 1 | 2 | 3 | 4 | 5 |
| How appropriate is the language? | 1 | 2 | 3 | 4 | 5 |

| | Score 4 | Score 3 | Score 2 | Score 1 |
|---|---|---|---|---|
| Audience and Purpose | Uses word choices and supporting details appropriate to the specified audience; clearly addresses writing prompt | Mostly uses word choices and supporting details appropriate to the specified audience; adequately addresses prompt | Uses some inappropriate word choices and details; addresses writing prompt | Uses inappropriate word choices and details; does not address writing prompt |
| Organization | Presents a clear, consistent organizational strategy | Presents a clear organizational strategy with few inconsistencies | Presents an inconsistent organizational strategy | Shows a lack of organizational strategy |
| Elaboration | Adequately supports the thesis; elaborates each idea; links all details to the thesis | Supports the thesis; elaborates most ideas; links most information to thesis | Partially supports the thesis; does not elaborate some ideas | Provides no thesis; does not elaborate ideas |
| Use of Language | Uses excellent sentence variety and vocabulary; includes very few mechanical errors | Uses adequate sentence variety and vocabulary; includes few mechanical errors | Uses repetitive sentence structure and vocabulary; includes some mechanical errors | Demonstrates poor use of language; includes many mechanical errors |

# Rubric for Evaluating a Persuasive Presentation

*Use the following rubric to assess evaluating persuasive messages.*

| Rating System | | |
|---|---|---|
| + = excellent | ✓ = average | — = weak |

**Content**
Determines the speaker's attitude _____
Listens for strong evidence _____
Considers sources of information _____
Distinguishes between fact and opinion _____
Evaluates reliability and accuracy of information _____
Distinguishes between entertainment, persuasion, and factual information _____

**Delivery**
Listen for logical organization _____
Recognizes persuasive techniques _____
Recognizes visual, auditory, and special effects _____
Responds constructively by questioning, challenging, or affirming _____
Recognizes the persuasive intent of the presentation _____
Ascertains the basic message of the presentation _____

**Evaluation Summary**
Persuasive techniques do not unduly influence evaluation _____
Sound reasoning is used to make a judgment about the presentation _____
A conclusion regarding the reliability of the presentation is reached _____
An appropriate evaluation of the presentation is made _____

# Rubric for Evaluating Media Messages

*Use the following rubric to assess evaluating media messages.*

| Rating System | | |
|---|---|---|
| + = excellent | ✓ = average | — = weak |

**Content**
Analyzes images _____
Analyzes text _____
Analyzes sound _____
Listens for strong evidence _____
Distinguishes between entertainment, persuasion, and factual information _____

**Delivery**
Recognizes persuasive techniques _____
Recognizes visual, auditory, and special effects _____
Analyzes effects _____
Identifies the techniques used to achieve media effects _____
Recognizes the intent of the message _____

**Evaluation Summary**
Persuasive techniques do not unduly influence evaluation _____
Effects and the techniques used to achieve them are considered _____
Sound reasoning is used to make a judgment about the message _____
A conclusion regarding the message is reached _____
An appropriate evaluation of the message is made _____

# Rubric for Evaluating Advertisements

*Use the following rubric to assess evaluating advertisements.*

| Rating System | | |
|---|---|---|
| + = excellent | ✓ = average | — = weak |

**Content**
Evaluates content _____
Challenges the claims and the logic _____
Considers sources of information _____
Distinguishes between facts, effects, and persuasive techniques _____

**Delivery**
Evaluates delivery _____
Recognizes persuasive techniques _____
Analyzes entertainment effects _____
Analyzes emotional effects _____
Recognizes the persuasive intent of the advertisement _____

**Evaluation Summary**
Persuasive techniques do not unduly influence evaluation _____
Sound reasoning is used to make a judgment about the advertisement _____
A conclusion regarding the advertisement is reached _____
An appropriate evaluation of the advertisement is made _____

# Rubric for Evaluating a Media Presentation

*Use the following rubric to assess evaluations of media presentations.*

**Rating System**

+ = excellent          ✓ = average          — = weak

**Content**
Analyzes the effects of images, text, and sound _____
Identifies techniques used to achieve effects _____
Evaluates the logic of the content _____
Distinguishes between entertainment, persuasion, and factual information _____

**Delivery**
Evaluates the logic of the organization _____
Recognizes persuasive techniques _____
Responds constructively by questioning, challenging, or affirming _____
Recognizes the intent of the presentation _____

**Evaluation Summary**
Effects and the techniques used to achieve them are considered _____
Sound reasoning is used to make a judgment about the presentation _____
A conclusion regarding the presentation is reached _____
An appropriate evaluation of the presentation is made _____

# Rubric for Giving and Receiving Oral Directions

*Use the following rubric to evaluate giving and receiving oral directions.*

| Rating System | | |
|---|---|---|
| + = excellent | ✓ = average | — = weak |

## Receiving Directions
Focuses on the speaker _____
Visualizes the information _____
Listens for key words _____
Takes notes or repeats aloud _____
Asks questions at the end _____
Restates the directions in own words _____
Executes all of the steps _____

## Giving Directions
Focuses on the person receiving the directions _____
Proceeds step-by-step _____
Provides visual clues _____
Restates the directions _____

## Evaluation Summary
Receiver understands the speaker's message and carries out the steps in order _____
Giver is patient and uses a step-by-step approach _____
Giver avoids adding any unnecessary details _____

# Rubric for Narrative Account

*Use the following rubric to evaluate narrative accounts.*

| Rating System | | |
|---|---|---|
| + = excellent | ✓ = average | — = weak |

**Content**
Establishes and maintains context _____
Develops a standard plot line and point of view _____
Establishes a central conflict _____
Includes sensory details and concrete language _____

**Delivery**
Uses appropriate verbal techniques _____
Uses appropriate nonverbal techniques _____
Presents events in chronological order _____
Exhibits a range of narrative devices, including naming specific narrative actions _____
Appeals to background and interests of the audience _____
Achieves a focused and coherent presentation _____

**Presentation Summary**
Attitude toward narrative is apparent and appropriate _____
Attitude toward the audience is apparent and appropriate _____
Preparation is evident and thorough _____
Organization is discernible and effective _____

# Rubric for Presenting a Proposal

Use the following rubric to evaluate presenting a proposal.

| Rating System | | |
|---|---|---|
| + = excellent | ✓ = average | — = weak |

### Content
Establishes and maintains context _____
Identifies the need for action _____
States a clear position regarding a course of action _____
Arranges details, descriptions, and examples persuasively _____

### Delivery
Uses appropriate verbal techniques _____
Uses appropriate nonverbal techniques _____
Organizes and presents the proposal effectively _____
Focuses on the audience _____
Addresses background and interests of the audience _____
Achieves a focused and coherent presentation _____

### Presentation Summary
Attitude toward the needed action is appropriate _____
Attitude toward the audience is apparent and appropriate _____
Preparation is evident and thorough _____
Organization is discernible and effective _____

# Rubric for Organizing and Delivering an Oral Summary

*Use the following rubric to evaluate organizing and delivering an oral summary.*

| Rating System | | |
|---|---|---|
| + = excellent | ✓ = average | — = weak |

### Content
Establishes and maintains context _____
Briefly states main idea _____
Includes the most significant details _____
Conveys a comprehensive understanding of the source _____

### Delivery
Uses appropriate verbal techniques _____
Uses appropriate nonverbal techniques _____
Organizes content _____
Addresses background and interests of the audience _____
Achieves a focused and coherent presentation _____

### Presentation Summary
Attitude toward the source is apparent and appropriate _____
Attitude toward the audience is apparent and appropriate _____
Preparation is evident and thorough _____
Organization is discernible and effective _____

# Rubric for Research Presentation

*Use the following rubric to evaluate research presentations.*

| Rating System | | |
|---|---|---|
| + = excellent | ✓ = average | — = weak |

### Content
Establishes and maintains context _____
Poses a consise question on a relevant topic _____
Addresses the topic completely and thoroughly _____
Draws from multiple authoritative sources _____
Supports the topic with facts, details, examples, and explanations _____
Cites reference sources appropriately _____

### Delivery
Uses appropriate verbal techniques _____
Uses appropriate nonverbal techniques _____
Uses an organizational structure that matches purpose and information _____
Presents appropriate visual aids _____
Achieves a focused and coherent presentation _____
Answers questions from the audience appropriately _____

### Presentation Summary
Attitude toward topic is apparent and appropriate _____
Clear and accurate perspectives are conveyed _____
Attitude toward the audience is apparent and appropriate _____
Preparation is evident and thorough _____
Organization is discernible and effective _____

# Rubric for Presenting Pros and Cons

*Use the following rubric to evaluate presenting pros and cons.*

| Rating System | | |
|---|---|---|
| + = excellent | ✓ = average | — = weak |

**Content**
Establishes and maintains context _____
Poses a well-worded question _____
States a each position clearly _____
Gives specific evidence for each side _____

**Delivery**
Uses appropriate verbal techniques _____
Uses appropriate nonverbal techniques _____
Uses an organizational structure that matches purpose and information _____
Engages the audience _____
Presents appropriate visual aids _____
Achieves a focused and coherent presentation _____

**Presentation Summary**
Attitude toward both sides of the topic is apparent and appropriate_____
Attitude toward the audience is apparent and appropriate_____
Preparation is evident and thorough_____
Organization is discernible and effective_____

# Listening and Speaking Progress Chart: Teacher Observation

**Directions to the teacher:** This chart is designed to help you track the progress of students' listening and speaking behavior. Write the students' names in the first column. Use the Key to record your observations for each behavior. Share your observations with students to help them recognize how their listening and speaking skills have progressed and to help them set goals for improving.

**Key** **P** = Proficient **I** = Improving **N** = Needs Attention

## Progress Chart: Listening

| Student's Name | Pays attention. | Listens with a purpose. | Is polite and does not interrupt. | Responds appropriately. | Asks questions clarify ideas. |
|---|---|---|---|---|---|
| | | | | | |
| | | | | | |
| | | | | | |
| | | | | | |
| | | | | | |
| | | | | | |
| | | | | | |
| | | | | | |
| | | | | | |
| | | | | | |
| | | | | | |

# Listening and Speaking Progress Chart: Teacher Observation

**Directions to the teacher:** This chart is designed to help you track the progress of students' listening and speaking behavior. Write the students' names in the first column. Use the Key to record your observations for each behavior. Share your observations with students to help them recognize how their listening and speaking skills have progressed and to help them set goals for improving.

**Key    P** = Proficient   **I** = Improving   **N** = Needs Attention

## Progress Chart: Speaking

| Student's Name | Enjoys speaking to a group. | Appears calm and confident. | Is prepared and knows material. | Uses body language and gestures effectively. | Uses visual aids effectively. |
|---|---|---|---|---|---|
| | | | | | |
| | | | | | |
| | | | | | |
| | | | | | |
| | | | | | |
| | | | | | |
| | | | | | |
| | | | | | |
| | | | | | |
| | | | | | |
| | | | | | |

# Performance Assessment: Scoring Models

The models of student work that follow are scored 1, 2, 3, or 4. In addition to rubrics, you may use these models as a guide when assessing your students' work.

# Scoring Model for Narration: Autobiographical Narrative

## Score 4

This writer presents an autobiographical narrative with a logical sequence of events in a well-elaborated, engaging style.

### Strong Points:

1. Engaging introduction
2. Clear and consistent narration
3. Sophisticated use of sensory imagery
4. Provides insight into character
5. Effective dialogue
6. Variety in sentence length and structure
7. No errors in grammar, punctuation, or spelling

## Buela

I remember the day very clearly. My eighth-grade sister was two years older than I. We had just walked home from the bus stop. We were hot, tired, and sweaty from the Texas sun beating down on us. As usual, the answering machine beeped annoyingly.

"Let's just wait until Mom gets home," my sister Yolanda said.

"No, you know how tired she is when she gets home. We better just play it now."

When we listened to the calls, the first two had hung up. When the third one came, my aunt's voice was on the phone.

"I just wanted to let you know that Grandma passed away. The funeral has not been set, but we will call you when we get the details."

My sister picked up the phone and called my father. We knew this would hurt him terribly. While Yolanda called my mother, I walked into the living room and turned on the television. I thought in my head, Buela's dead. I didn't know how to react so I just focused on the television.

The next day we went to L— (a little town south of here) to meet my father's family. I didn't realize that I would never see Buela again. Since my aunt lived at her apartment with her, she greeted us at the door. As I walked into Buela's room, my eyes filled with tears. I saw pictures of her with all of her twenty-one grandchildren. On her bed were her glasses. On the counter her many rosaries shined brightly in the sun. My mother guided me to the couch, and I cried in her shoulder until my eyes were heavy and puffy.

The next day was Buela's funeral. She had a beautiful white casket trimmed with brass and the corners had a picture of the Virgin Mary. We met up with our cousins whom we hadn't seen in two years. I met people who I didn't even know held the Mendez name. I entered the small place and walked slowly toward my abuela. The air felt cold and smelled stale. They played soft classical music in the background. Each step I took seemed heavier than the first. Her hair was nicely done and her lips were painted a rosy red. Her skin was a combination of pale and dark. I slowly bent down to touch her. Her arm was cold and hard. The funeral was beautifully done in Spanish.

Sometimes when I think of Buela, I want to cry, but then I realize that she is now at peace. She always talked about God and angels, and now she is with them.

# Scoring Model for Narration: Autobiographical Narrative

## Score 3

This writer presents an engaging autobiographical narrative with clear organization and vivid description.

### Strong Points:

1. Engaging introduction
2. Clear sequence of events
3. Consistent narrative point of view
4. Effective word choices and vivid descriptive details that develop plot

### Problem Points:

1. Little variety in sentence structure
2. Sparse dialogue
3. Some errors of punctuation
4. Abrupt conclusion

## A Close Call

Wet, scared, and excited, that's how I feel when I ride a four wheeler behind someone who holds your life in his hands. Four wheeling is a real adventure.

There's nothing I like better than to go riding with my dad and my brother Tyler. One day we were slicing through the snow like nothing else when a deer ran by right in front of us. My dad tried dodging and almost flipped the four wheeler. That's what can happen sometimes.

On one ride my dad and I were approaching a huge field, and when my dad was turning he almost flipped again. My brother was doing 360s and he asked my dad if he could do the same. My dad said "Of course! I created the 360!" We raced gaining speed every minute, then we hit a patch of slick ice like a bullet out of a gun. My dad started turning the machine but we started spinning round and round. We went faster and faster then we hit a grass patch and flipped. I flew headfirst over my dad, spinning and flipping.

I don't remember hitting the ground. Everything went black for a few seconds. I looked up just in time to see the four wheeler land on my dad. I couldn't believe what I saw. My heart jumped in my throat. I got up and ran over to him and tried lifting it. I struggled but couldn't budge that huge monster. I yelled to Tyler but he couldn't hear me so I told my dad that I was somehow going to hold it up enough for him to get out. I strained and strained with all my strength and finally lifted the four wheeler just enough. My dad jumped out. I dropped it, ran over to him and talked to him for a minute.

My uncle saw what happened and zoomed over to help. We picked up the four wheeler and then helped my dad over to sit down on it. My dad had a big cut on his leg and nothing more. What a relief! All that happened to me was a scratch on my helmet.

I had to drive home because of my dad's leg.

# Scoring Model for Narration: Autobiographical Narrative

## Score 2

While this writer presents a clear sequence of events, the narrative's weaknesses outweigh its strengths.

### Strong Points:

1. Clear sequence of events
2. Includes some dialogue

### Problem Points:

1. Uninspiring opening and conclusion
2. Little plot and character development
3. Insufficient dialogue
4. Limited variety in sentence structure
5. Lackluster details and word choices
6. Errors of punctuation, spelling, grammar, and usage

## Flying

My father and me arrived at the pilot's house for a trip in a small plane. The pilot came over to us and let us in the plane after he had finished untying it from its bay, he started the engines and set a corse for the end of the lake. He turned the plane around to face the other side, and increased throtle.

At speeds aproaching 60 miles an hour the pilot brought the altatude control backwards therefore bringing the plane into an asent. As soon as we were in the air he asked us where we wanted to go, my father answered and then the pilot changed corse. He flew us over the middle school, and our property. Then he set a corse for a few interesting places he wanted to fly, he landed in those places and in one of them we refuled. He explained, "That area is a good area for flight training.

Then he took the plane into a climb again, then we followed another plane, the pilot talked to the other plane on his comunication radio. He said "Fly towards that lake. He periodicaly said more specific parts of the lake. He said, "Congratulations!" and I wondered if he would let me put the plane into a roll or loop. In the small plane we flew for another few hours. When we landed we said, Thanks. to the pilot, and then we went home.

# Scoring Model for Narration: Autobiographical Narrative

## Score 1

This writer's attempts to write an autobiographical narrative are unsuccessful.

### Problem Points:

1. Unclear narrative purpose
2. No particular organizing principle
3. Sparse details
4. Insufficient dialogue and elaboration
5. Uninteresting word choices
6. No conclusion
7. Many mechanical errors

### Stiches

It all started when my frend Eddie came over for super we went out to the play room then we got on the skatebord and I went around the play room a cuple times. Eddie and me were runing and playing hard when my mother yelled out stop runing before you get hert then it hapened right into the arm of the chair I ran and spilt my hed wide opin. My aunt Carla called Rescu. When they came they checked my sins and put me on the strecher, then they put me in the back of the rescue unit, off to the emergcy room we went to put stiches in my forhed. While I was in the unit a man was teling me stories about kids getting hurt, then he pulled out this blue bear from a cuboards and said, this bear would like to be your friend. I still have that bear to this day that man was right, it did make me feel better. The man had to try and keep me awake so I would not go unconcus, they also put an oxigin mask on my face that was realy weird. I did not like that at all so if you ever get hurt don't be afraid because these people are real nice and they treat you realy well. To help this keep hapening you can donate your stufed animals that you don't want to the police stasion or rescu they both do this to keep children not to be afraid when some thing hapens to them.

# Scoring Model for Description: Descriptive Composition

## Score 4

This writer presents a clearly focused description with effective details and rich sensory language.

### Strong Points:

1. Powerful opening paragraph
2. Fully elaborated, memorable details
3. Rich sensory images and figurative language
4. Effective organization
5. Good sentence variety

## Our Tree

Green flows everywhere in our backyard until it hits the maple tree that sizzles in the sun and overpowers everything around it. Even though the tree grows high into the sky, its tangled limbs and stiff base are cemented in the ground by muscular roots. The maple stands alone next to a swamp. The two sit so close together they're like the best of friends. A sleepy green hill makes the final member of the group. With the tangled maple as leader, this team borders our land and separates us from our neighbors.

The bark of the maple is a surprise the moment you touch it—a combination of bumpy and smooth. Because another tree leans on it, all the branches explode from one side, leaving the other side bare. They look as though they want to escape from the other trees.

From the branches, blazing red and fiery orange leaves pop out everywhere, and behind them, pale green and sunshine yellow leaves fill in the rest of the tree. Here and there dead brown leaves mingle with the others to remind us of what is in store. Already the leaves are falling as the air grows colder and winter draws near. The tree will soon be bare, but for now it burns the ground and lightens the sky for everyone to see.

# Scoring Model for Description: Descriptive Composition

## Score 3

This writer presents a well-organized, memorable description with interesting details.

### Strong Points:

1. Effective organization
2. Interesting details

### Problem Points:

1. Limited sensory language
2. Few visual details
3. Limited vocabulary
4. Sentence structure errors

## A Work of Art

For generations, the women in my family kept a quilt. The quilt was kept in the third house of the Morris family in Denver. The quilt was priceless, and everybody admired it.

My great, great, great, great . . . great grandmother started it with a first patch. The first patch that she sewed was a star. She later passed the work to her daughter, and her daughter passed it to her daughter, and so on.

When I first saw the quilt, I was seven years old. I was so happy I cried. I was stunned with joy as were my mom and dad. They had seen the quilt before, but my sister has never seen it because she was born after we moved away.

The quilt had over 350 patches of all different materials and different pictures. Each patch represented a story of something that happened during that time.

My aunt's house held the quilt, she was the oldest and most trusted member of the family. She took very good care of the quilt. It was kept in a glass case with a lock on it. The glass was hard to break. My aunt had a great pride and protected it very well.

When we left Denver, the quilt was still at my aunt's. Today I have no idea where it is. It could be with her still, or it could be somewhere else. I hope it is still with her so that, when I go back to Colorado I can see it, and if I have a daughter my daughter can make a patch.

# Scoring Model for Description: Descriptive Composition

## Score 2

This writer presents a disorganized description with limited elaboration; its strong points are outweighed by its problem points.

### Strong Points:

1. Good visual details
2. Simple sentence structures

### Problem Points:

1. Poor organization
2. Distracting grammatical errors
3. Uninteresting word choices
4. Spelling errors
5. Limited elaboration
6. No introduction; abrupt ending

### The Dress for Me

First, in every weding, you need to decide on your wedding dress. My dream weding dress has beeds all over the train and the gown and the top part of the gown has a design of waves moving and the train of the gown has a little design on the end of it. The vail the part of the dress that goes over your head sits on your head like a crown and then the rest of it goes down the back of your head. On the gown there is also embroderie. Then the part of the vail that sits on your forhead is lined with lace, or beeds that look like pearls, and with leaves that hock into your hair. The dress will be long with a train that goes way back. I will have a flower girl hold it. That is what my wedding dress would look like.

# Scoring Model for Description: Descriptive Composition

## Score 1

This writer's attempts to write an effective description are unsuccessful.

## Problem Points:

1. Flat language
2. Lack of sensory details and figurative language
3. Simplistic sentence structure
4. Distracting errors of grammar, usage, spelling, and punctuation
5. No introduction or conclusion

### My Tree

Deep in the woods behind my house there it Stands the tall, thin Oak tree! My tree lives next to 3 other oak trees, 2 pine trees and a big rock lays between 2 of the oak trees. My tree is surrounded by grass and weeds. My tree is in a gully like type thing. My tree is all differant sizes and shapes, it goes left, right, left, and then right again. Its long and Skiny.

# Scoring Model for Persuasion: Persuasive Composition

## Score 4

This writer makes a clear position statement and provides good organization, elaboration, and word choice.

## Strong Points:

1. Strong position statement in introduction
2. Clear, consistent organizational strategy
3. Forceful persuasive arguments
4. Examples and other supporting details
5. Persuasive words that appeal to the audience
6. Transitions to connect ideas
7. Conclusion that sums up the issue
8. Few mechanical errors

## The Television Question

Until the television was invented, families spent their time doing different activities. Now most families stay home and watch TV. Watching TV risks the family's health, reduces the children's study time and is a bad influence on young minds. Watching television can be harmful.

The most important reason why watching TV is bad is because the viewers get less exercise. For example, instead of watching their favorite show, people could exercise for 30 minutes. If people spent less time watching TV and more time exercising, then they could have a healthier body. My mother told me a story about a man who died of a heart attack because he was out of shape from watching television all the time. Obviously, watching TV can put a person's health in danger.

Furthermore, watching television reduces children's study time. For example, children would spend more time studying if they didn't watch television. If students spent more time studying at home, then they would make better grades at school. Last week I had a major test in science, but I didn't study because I started watching a movie. I was not prepared for the test and my grade reflected my lack of studying. Indeed, watching television is bad because it can hurt a student's grades.

Finally, watching TV can be a bad influence on children. For example, some TV shows have inappropriate language and too much violence. If children watch programs that use bad language and show violence, then they may start repeating these actions because they think the behavior is "cool." In fact, it has been proven that children copy what they see on TV. Clearly, watching TV is bad for children and it affects children's behavior.

In conclusion, watching television is a bad influence for these reasons: It reduces people's exercise time and students' study time, and it shows children inappropriate behavior. Therefore, people should take control of their lives and stop allowing television to harm them.

# Scoring Model for Persuasion: Persuasive Composition

## Score 3

This writer presents a well-elaborated persuasive composition with a clear organizational strategy and some elaboration.

### Strong Points:

1. Clear position statement in introduction
2. Arguments that appeal to the audience and serve the persuasive purpose
3. Clear organizational strategy with some inconsistencies
4. Elaboration and support for the writer's position
5. Some transitions

### Problem Points:

1. Lacks strong word choice
2. Minor organizational problems
3. Some mechanical errors

## Does TV Hurt or Help?

Although television could be bad for the health of many peple there are some good reasons why television is good. Entertainment, learning information, and potential family time together are some reasons why TV can be good. Certainly television helps today's families.

My first reasons for watching television are entertainment and education. For example there are cartoons for children so they can be entertained while their mother is busy. Furthermore there are many educational TV games for all ages.

Furthermore learning information can be interesting. For example there are many channels where you could learn about different things and places. Channel 8 is a very interesting channel, it's a great tool for learning. This channel shows other places, continents, states and cultures. There are also channels that teach how to cook different foods. In addition one of the most important features of television is the news. It is important for people of all ages to stay informed.

Finally my last reason is potential family time together. Watching TV could be the only time when a family can be together. It is also good to relax and watch TV after a busy day. There are many programs or movies for the family to enjoy together. Families need a time to come together and television offers them that opportunity.

For these reasons watching television could be a good idea. Entertainment, learning information, and quality family time make television a good influence in the home. I think watching television is a good idea.

# Scoring Model for Persuasion: Persuasive Composition

## Score 2

Although the writer has organized the ideas in this persuasive composition, its weaknesses outweigh its strengths.

### Strong Points:

1. Good organization
2. Some arguments that serve the persuasive purpose

### Problem Points:

1. Weak opening and closing position statements
2. Little consideration of audience
3. Digression from main points; faulty logic
4. No transitions
5. Rushed final paragraphs
6. Many mechanical errors

### Is TV Good or Bad for Families?

I think spending too much time waching television is a horible thing to do. There is violence and other bad things on tv. Millions of Americans don't get enough exercise because of waching too much television, many people spend almost half of there days watching television.

The most important ting is that tv these days has a great amount of violence, profanety, and crime. Millions of children wach these things on tv that are bad. I believe television is horible because of the violence is shows.

Many people do not get enouf exercise because of waching too much tv. People just don't spend enough time working out. There are other things that you can do instead of waching television. There are many healthier things to do with a good day than waching tv. That is another reason why waching tlevision is a horible thing to do.

Many Americans spend over half their lifes waching tv, I once herd of a man who died at age of 30 because he hardly evr did anything besides wach tv. Too much time is spend by people waching tv and their lives are being shortened because of tv.

Waching too much tv is a serious habit. There are too many other healthier things to be doing. The content of television is also creating problems. It is time to turn tv off.

# Scoring Model for Persuasion: Persuasive Composition

## Score 1

This writer's attempts to write a persuasive composition are unsuccessful.

### Problem Points:

1. Little attention to audience or persuasive purpose
2. Lacks organizational strategy
3. Lacks persuasive arguments and illustrations
4. Weak word choices
5. Little elaboration
6. Unclear and confusing writing
7. Numerous spelling and punctuation errors
8. Many grammatical errors

## Good to Watch

I'm going to give 3 good convinsing reason for watching telvision. My first reason for watching telvision is whats happening to peoples life. The second good reason for watching telvision is you finds stuff you don't know about. The third good reason for watching telvision is your faverite TV shows for example good news and shows about church and singing. Bad things are happining to peoples life everyday, they are hurting they self everyday, that why people look at telvision.

For instance, people need to watach TV. That how they knows more about what goes on like violence and game shows that comes on to help you understand better the things that are happining to people's lifes for example, my second reason you find out things you didn't know about. For instance while looking at telvision you might hear or see something that you have never seen before intil you have watched television. You find out things you didn't know about. Finally you watch your favorite TV shows, for example one about church and singing. Telvision is good for people to waatch. People should watch telvision.

# Scoring Model for Narration: Short Story

## Score 4

This writer presents a story that is consistently organized and logical with interesting detail and character development.

## Strong Points:

1. Engaging and entertaining plot
2. Logical sequence of events
3. Consistent and interesting character development
4. Appropriate word choice and tone for the story's theme
5. Varied sentence structure
6. Very few or no errors in spelling and grammar

### Why the Great Salt Lake is Salty

Once upon a time in Utah lived a family. There was a mother and father, and two boys, Bob and Bill. Bob, the oldest, was always rude and very lazy. Bill, on the other hand, was kind and did all of the family's housework.

Years passed and the boys grew up. Bob was rich and lived by himself in a mansion. Bill grew up to be a farmer who raised cattle and corn to feed his family. One day the corn was all gone so he went to his brother. "Bob, can you please give me a bag of corn? I have run out of food for my family and we will soon starve."

Bob responded with "Bill, I work for my food. Maybe you should do the same."

So Bill left his brother's house, worried and ashamed. He walked down the street and observed an old man holding wooden boards. Bill, being kind as usual, asked the man if he could carry the boards. The man, grateful, agreed quickly. Soon Bill was at the man's house. The man thanked him and went inside. He came out with a corn grinder.

He said, "This is a magical corn grinder. You can ask for anything and it will give it to you. You turn the handle around once, and whatever you want will come out. When you move it around twice, it will stop."

Bill thanked him and ran home so he could try it. When he went home, he said to the grinder, "I would like some corn."

He turned the grinder around once, and suddenly corn came flooding out. Soon it was covering the table. When he turned it around a second time, the corn magically stopped. Bill was thankful and soon was asking for more things: tools, furniture, clothing, and many other things. He gave these things to his neighbors and soon people were talking about his generosity.

Bob soon heard about this and became jealous. He went to Bill's house and asked about the gifts. Bill told him the story and Bob said, "May I see this magical grinder?"

Bill came over with it. He handed it to Bob and said, "Be careful. This means everything to me."

Bob, however, grabbed it and suddenly ran out of the door. He ran to the Great Lake, jumped into a waiting boat, and rowed away. He had been rowing a while when he became hungry. He pulled a tomato out of his pack. Taking a bite, he said, "This tomato tastes very dull. I need some salt."

He took the grinder out and said, "Salt!"

Then he turned the handle once around and salt began to flood out. Seeing how much salt it produced, Bob shouted, "Stop! No more salt!" But the salt kept pouring out. Angrily, Bob shouted again, "Stop! Stop! I command you!" but the salt only flowed faster from the magic grinder.

Soon the boat was flooded with salt and capsized. Bob was thrown into the water. The grinder was thrown to the bottom of the deep lake. The grinder is there still today and Bob has not been seen ever again. That is why the Great Salt Lake is salty.

# Scoring Model for Narration: Short Story

## Score 3

This writer presents an engaging and sometimes witty story, with only minor errors in punctuation, grammar, and spelling.

### Strong Points:

1. Engaging introduction
2. Clear plot development
3. Realistic dialogue
4. Few errors in grammar, punctuation, and spelling

### Problem Points:

1. Rushed sequence of events
2. Insufficient character development
3. Imagery lacks detail

### In Orbit

Far, far away in outer space was a planet named Zippity-do-da where an evil creature named Zunilda lived. All the other creatures on the planet hated her. That made Zunilda sad, so she decided to try something new. She jumped into her spacemobile and traveled to planet Earth. When she got to Earth, she heard the Earthlings talking about Disneyland and the wonderful characters there who made people happy. So Zunilda bought a map on the corner of
Hollywood and Vine and found her way to Disneyland. When she got there, she kidnaped some of the characters and took them back to Zippity-do-da.

"When everybody sees what I've got, they'll want to be my friend," Zunilda thought happily. But to Zunilda's dismay, the creatures of Zippity-do-da were angry with her because she had stolen Earth's happiness.

Meanwhile, back on Earth, everyone was trying to find the Disney characters. All of a sudden, they spotted Pluto crying.

"Pluto, do you know where the other Disney characters are?" they asked.

"I don't know," he said. "They were here just a minute ago. Now they are gone."

Then a man came running toward Pluto. "I know what happened to the Disney Characters! An evil creature took them away in a space mobile."

"Where were they going?" cried Pluto.

The license plate said Zippity-do-da," the man answered.

When Pluto heard that, he ran to Launch Mountain, climbed in one of the cars, and flew off to Zippity-do-da. When he got there, he asked where he could find the evil creature.

"You must mean Zunilda. She has your friends. We'll help you get them back," they said, and they flew off with Pluto to zunilda's castle. They searched the castle for the Disney characters and found them in a cage.

How can I get you guys out? Where's the key?" Pluto asked.

Mickey replied, "She locked us in here with a key, so there's gotta be a key somewhere." Pluto and the others searched, but they couldn't find the key. Suddenly, they could hear footsteps coming toward them. Every body ran to hide, but it was too late. Zunilda saw them, but Pluto saw the key hanging around her neck.

How was Pluto going to get the key off Zunilda's neck? Pluto had an idea. He began to run around the room in circles with Zunilda right behind him. He ran around and around until Zunilda became so dizzy that she fell to the floor with a crash. Pluto grabbed the key, and he unlocked the door to the cage.

As soon as the other Disney characters and Pluto were safe outside the castle, they ran to the spaceship. They jumped in, but Zunilda was hot on their heels. She jumped into her spacemobile and flew after them. As they neared Saturn, a nearbye planet, Pluto saw that Zunilda was gaining on them. He thought that if his first plan worked once, shouldn't it work again? They began to fly around Saturn with Zunilda right behind them. Pluto saw his chance and hit the brake. Zunilda flew by them, and Pluto sped back to Earth. To this day you can still see the rings Zunilda left behind!

Pluto and his friends landed safely on Earth. And back on Zippity-do-da the creatures were so glad that Zunilda was gone that they renamed their planet after their hero, Pluto.

And if you listen carefully to the winds, you can hear the creatures of Pluto singing their favorite song, "Zippity-do-da, Zippity-ay. My oh my, what a wonderful day . . ."

# Scoring Model for Narration: Short Story

## Score 2

This writer presents a long-winded story with an interesting introduction and conclusion but a confusing and illogical plot.

### Strong Points:

1. Effective use of dialogue
2. Contains some interesting details
3. Good use of language

### Problem Points:

1. Weak plot construction
2. Abrupt ending
3. Little or no character development
4. Numerous errors in spelling, punctuation, and grammar

## Sam's vacation

Ring! The eighth period bell of the last day of school rings. Rick, Imelda, Sam, and Irma are all best friends and have no plans for the summer. The first day of summer was finaly here, but as any four teenagers that are out of high school have no way to celebrate the coming of the summer. Secretly Imelda liked Rick and Sam liked Irma. Sam and Imelda thought long of a place to kick back and relax and soon they thought of a wonderful fun place, but first they had to put all their fast food working, babysitting, car washing money together and by 4 plane tickets to Tampa for 2 long relaxing weeks.

The next day, Imelda and Sam told Irma and Rick there plane ride to a fun 2 weeks was takeing off tomorrow. They were so excited but the only problem was they only had one day to pack which was cayos. The day of the big trip arived and the plane left at eight o'clock that morning so they woke up extra early, it was about 7:45 and when the flite attendent annoynced over the intercom may I have your atention, flite 402 will be posponed until two o clock later this afternoon sorry for this inconvenence and thank you.

The 4 didn't mind so they went to go eat at a little cafay located in the airport. As they were sitting in the cafay, Imelda said "What if something goes wrong on our flite? Sam told her not to worry and not to think things like that. Two o'clock came and the four were waiting patientley in the loby eager to start there vacation when the flite attendent announced that flight four zero two to Tampa was bording.

Sam and Rick pushed through the large crowd dragging Imelda and Irma behind. The trip there took forever I guess because they were so eager to start there vacation. But the way back was long but full of memories. Sam was so tired he slept right when he got home when he woke up the next morning his mom asked him how things were. Sam replied The day we arrived mom, was so cool we were greeted by nice people who gave us lemonade. The first week we relaxed and went swiming in the pool. Then Irma told us about a beutiful place to go hiking so we hired a guide and went hiking. The seenery was amazing, then we took a nice walk by the river where Irma and I had our first kiss! We spent the rest of our stay there partying.

Sam's mom interupted What are you talking about? Sam replied Oh my gosh, It was all a dream! I should of known that because a dream vacation with Irma could never happen!

# Scoring Model for Narration: Short Story

## Score 1

This writer presents a story with few details and weak mechanics.

### Problem Points:

1. Poorly developed plot
2. Few and unclear descriptive details
3. Little character development
4. Consistently poor sentence structure
5. Spelling mistakes that often obscure meaning
6. Limited vocabulary

### Cats and Dogs

Once upon a time a long time ago cats were larger then dogs and you maybe thinking this is wired but is true. Deep in the Moave desert live a uge cat named Morgan and a small dog named Grover and they dispised each other because they were cat and dog. Morgan would all ways play meen jokes on Grover and she would all ways act as if she was going to be nice and share her food and then she punce on Grover and make him cry Grover got tird of the jokes so he went to the magishunn so he could get reveng when he went to the magishun and explaned his problem the magishun gave him a magikal posson that would shrink cats so the following day Grover heded over to Morgans house with the posson descized as milk so Morgan drank the milk suspenciously and all of a sudden his head shrunk as well as his paws then came his legs. No you and all your cat friends will be small for live Grover screemed.

# Scoring Model for Research: Research Report

## Score 4

This writer presents a clear, well-organized research report with a strong thesis statement, sound facts and examples, and complete citations.

### Strong Points:

1. Clearly stated thesis
2. Facts and details to support each main point
3. Accurate, complete citations identifying sources
4. Information presented in logical order, emphasizing details of central importance
5. Clear conclusions
6. Information gathered from a variety of sources
7. Overall fluency
8. Few mechanical errors

## Susan Brownell Anthony

Susan Brownell Anthony deserves a place in our women's Hall of Fame. On November 5, 1877 Susan B. Anthony took action that would later change the lives of women everywhere. At 7:00 A.M., she marched up to the polls in Rochester, New York, defiantly registered to vote, and cast her ballot for Ulysses S. Grant for president. By breaking the law that prohibited women from voting, she hoped that she would also break the powerful gender barrier. (Anderson 76) For her actions that day, Susan B. Anthony was arrested and fined $100. Americans today can appreciate her courage at challenging a law that she believed was wrong.

One reason Susan B. Anthony is so important is because of her outstanding temperance work, trying to ban alcohol. Anthony joined a temperance group called the Rochester Daughters of Temperance. They wanted to protect women and children from alcoholic husbands and fathers. Later Anthony and some followers formed the Woman's New York State Temperance Society. As the secretary of the new society, she attended a temperance convention in 1852 at Albany, New York. When she attempted to speak she was told, "The ladies have been invited to listen and learn and not to speak." (Smith 306) However, this little incident would not stop Susan B. Anthony.

Another example of why Susan Brownell Anthony deserves a place in the women's Hall of Fame is because of her hard work in the anti-slavery campaigns. She organized the National Women's Loyal League. Their goal was to have the constitution abolish slavery. In 1851, Anthony went to Syracuse to attend a series of anti-slavery meetings. A decade before the Civil War, she traveled as an agent for the American Anti-Slavery Society. Anthony conducted many campaigns against slavery. She was devoted to the anti-slavery movement, serving from 1856 to the outbreak of the Civil War in 1861. After many years against slavery she still did not think that she had done enough. (Anderson 180)

The most significant reason why Susan B. Anthony is such a great woman in history is because of her endurance, hard work, and sacrifice for women's rights. Her work for women's rights began in 1851, when she met Elizabeth Cady Stanton. From 1854–1860, she petitioned demanding women's rights to own property, and of their children to gain custody after a divorce. Anthony focused mainly on the constitutional amendment for women's suffrage, or the right to vote. In 1872, she demanded that women be given the same rights that had been extended to the black males under the 14th and 15th amendments. During 1868–1870, she published the newspaper the *Revolution*, which focused on injustices suffered by women. Anthony became the president of the National American Woman Suffrage Association and served eight years. In 1905, she visited President Theodore Roosevelt to urge him to support women's suffrage. After 50 years of leading the women's rights movement, Susan Brownwell Anthony retired. In 1920, the 19th Amendment granted the vote to women, but Anthony did not live to see it. She was described as the "Napoleon" of the suffrage movement. (Smith 118)

As you can see Susan Brownell Anthony was a very courageous woman. She played a very important part in history. If it was not for her, women would not be able to vote today. Anthony is a true hero because she did what she believed was right, no matter what the consequences.

## Works Cited

Anderson, Noah. *Susan B. Anthony: A Life.* Chicago, IL: Millstone Press, 1997.

Dudley, Andrea. *The Woman Suffrage Movement.* Los Angeles, CA: Arbor Publications, 1985.

Smith, Nicole. *The Life and Works of Susan B. Anthony.* New York, NY: Clark University Press, 1991.

# Scoring Model for Research: Research Report

## Score 3

This writer presents a well-organized research report with minor citation problems.

### Strong Points:

1. Clearly-stated thesis
2. Information well organized by chronology
3. Facts and details that support thesis
4. Good sentence variety
5. Information gathered from a variety of sources

### Problem Points:

1. Citations lack page references and alphabetical order in list
2. Weak conclusion
3. Some grammatical and mechanical errors
4. Some run-on sentences and fragments

## Thomas Jefferson

Out of all the people involved in the American Revolution, Thomas Jefferson is the most interesting. Jefferson was not only the President of the United States but also a farmer, lawyer, lawmaker, architect, inventor, archaeologist, and musician.

As stated in *The World Book Encyclopedia* Thomas Jefferson was born on April 13, 1743 in Goochland County, Virginia. He was the third child and grew up with six sisters and one brother. Jefferson was 14 years old when his father died. Cited in *The Importance of Thomas Jefferson,* when Jefferson was five, his parents hired a tutor to teach him mathematics, reading, and writing. At nine he was studying Latin. As a child, Jefferson liked hiking in the woods in Virginia. It was on one of these nature walks that Jefferson came upon the hilltop where he would one day build his famous home—Monticello.

Jefferson was outgoing and friendly. According to Vincent Sheean, "He was over six feet tall when he was seventeen years old—a rather awkward boy, with carroty red hair and freckles, a pointed nose and chin. You would never have called him handsome and yet his keen gray eyes and generally alert personality made him attractive to most people." (Nardo) In 1760, when he was seventeen, Jefferson enrolled in the College of William and Mary.  Jefferson finished college in 1762 and went on to study law.

Thomas Jefferson had a number of occupations in his life. According to *The Remarkable Jefferson Man of Many Faces.* He served as governor of Virginia and represented the new U.S. government in France. In June 1776, he wrote the Declaration of Independence as a member of the committee named to draft it. In 1800, he was nominated for President. Cited in the Internet source http://www.whitehouse.gov/Wh/glimpse/presidents/html/tj3.html when Jefferson assumed the presidency, he slashed Army and Navy expenditures, cut the budget, and reduced the national dept by a third. Jefferson acquired the Louisiana Territory from Napoleon in 1803.

In 1772, Jefferson married Martha Wayles Skelton, the daughter of a lawyer and they settled at Monticello, the home Jefferson designed and built between 1768 and 1809. They had one son and five daughters. Mrs. Jefferson died in 1782. Jefferson never remarried.

Jefferson was also an inventor, designer, creator, and architect of many things. In the book *Thomas Jefferson and his World* it states that Jefferson designed the Virginia State capitol in Richmond. He invented the polygraph machine, which copied letters, and designed the dumbwaiter, which brought things up from the cellar. The quartet stand, designed by Jefferson, held sheet music for four musicians (Jefferson played the violin). Jefferson designed a plow. He imported trees and plants from all over the world. Jefferson established the Library of Congress in 1800 and in time, the Library of Congress grew into the largest library in the world.

On July 4, 1826, exactly 50 years after the Declaration of Independence was approved. Jefferson died at Monticello after a short illness. The words that Jefferson wrote for his grave marker say: "Here was buried Thomas Jefferson, author of the Declaration of Independence, of the statue of Virginia for religious freedom, and the father of the University of Virginia." these were accomplishments that he thought were higher than being president of the United States. (Moscow)

In conclusion, Jefferson was a man of many talents and interests. That is why I chose this famous person to research.

## Works Cited

Scher, Linda. "The Remarkable Jefferson: Man of Many Faces." *Kids Discover*.
    Volume 8, Issue 1. January, 1998. Pages 2, 3, and 17.
Moscow, Henry. *Thomas Jefferson and his World.* New York, NY: American
    Heritage Publishing Co, Inc. 1960.
Nardo, Dan. *The Importance of Thomas Jefferson.* San Diego, CA: Lucent
    Books, Inc., 1993.
Cunningham, Noble. "Thomas Jefferson." *The World Book Encyclopedia*
"Thomas Jefferson."
    www.whitehouse.gov/Wh/glimpse/presidents/html/tj3.htm.

# Scoring Model for Research: Research Report

## Score 2

Although this writer provides an engaging opening, this research report's weaknesses outweigh its strengths.

### Strong Points:

1. Engaging opening
2. Introductory thesis
3. Explanation and interpretation of some information

### Problem Points:

1. No citations to support information
2. Insufficient sentence variety
3. Inconsistent, weak organization
4. Many mechanical errors
5. Excessive use of exclamation marks

## Mae Carol Jemison

"3 . . . 2 . . . 1 . . . BLAST OFF"! September 12 1992. History was in making, Mae Carol Jemison was becoming the first African-American to enter space. What an acomplishment! All of her study and training were finally paid off! Mae and the 14 others were probably very proud of theirselves. What she did stregthend the African-American communitys. She is a great roll modle and deserves our Women's Hall of Fame.

Mae Carol Jemison was born on October 17, 1956 in Decatur, Alabama. In her family, she was the youngest of 3. Her parents supported and encouraged Mae very much. she was 16 years old when she graduated and she erned a chemical engineer degree from Stanford in 1977. then she earned a medical degree from Cornell university in 1981. Chicago is her hometown.

Mae Jemison deserves the Women's hall of fame because of her hard work, she worked so hard in school, she went to Stanford and Cornell! She can also speak fluent Russan, Japanese, Swahili.

Also she is a great helping and caring person. She was an area peace core medical officer. She said that she wants to improve health care in west Africa. She also encourages women and minoritys to enter scientific fields. This is probably why she is a member of the asociation for the advancement of science. Dr. Jemison also worked CIGNA healthplans of California. But these are nothing compared to this.

Mae Jemison flew into space! she was the first black female astranomer to go into space, she spent over 240 hours in space on the spacecraft Endeavor. In space, she did all kinds of labs. Mae and 14 others were chosen by NASA to go into space out of 2,000 peoples. She was accepted in NASA's astranaut program in 1987. She resigned from NASA in 1993 to persue her personal goals.

Well, Mae Jemison is more than just a person who works all the time, she has a life also. Her hobies are photografy, forn languages, and a great skier! her 2 cats Sneeze and Little Mama.

So these reasons why Mae Carol Jemison deserves a place in the Women's hall of Fame. On top of all that, she flew into space. I think her wonderful life should be in the hall of Fame as a roll modle for people. I will be very disapointed if she is not elected.

# Scoring Model for Research: Research Report

## Score 1

This writer's attempts to present a research report are unsuccessful.

### Problem Points:

1. No thesis statement
2. Information lacks clear focus
3. Insufficient sentence variety
4. Weak organization
5. Little interpretation or synthesis of information
6. Incomplete information and ideas
7. Numerous spelling, punctuation, and grammatical errors
8. No citations to support factual information

## Susan B. Anthony

Let me introduce you to a American women Susan Brownell Anthony. She was born in Adams Masachuesets in 1820, secund of eight childrin. When she was 15 she became a teacher inspired by her father. when she was thirtie and got womens rights. Here is why I thick she should be in the women's hall of fame at our school.

One reason is becus of her curage to stand up and fight for rights. When she meets Elizabeth Stanton the two got started in womens rights to get women to vote. They publish a newspaper it was on injustices to women, and They started the womens sufrage movement.

Another reason becus of her bravery to vote illegaly. When she was 52 she was finned a $100 dollars but she refused and was arrested and taken to jale then she died alittle bit later peacfully at her home in Rochester New York. In 1919 congress approved the 19 amendment for women to vote. Susan was against a lot of other things she also did't like alkahol and she did't like slavery that's why she was in the loyal league against slavery.

# Scoring Model for Response to Literature

## Score 4

This writer presents a thoughtful, well-organized response to literature with compelling details and appropriate examples.

## Strong Points:

1. Well-written introduction with sufficient background information and clear thesis
2. Logical pattern of organization
3. Insightful explanations supported by precise, well-chosen examples
4. Clear connections to the overall focus
5. Fluent sentence structure and smooth transitions
6. Few mechanical errors

### Honor in *The Black Cauldron*

Lloyd Alexander's novel, *The Black Cauldron*, is a fantasy about tests and triumphs. In this story a small group of people search for an evil cauldron to destroy it and keep it from the hands of Arawn, a dark leader who seeks to control the land of Prydain. The different characters in *The Black Cauldron* have different ideas about honor. Three main characters with definite ideas about honor are Ellidyr, Adaon, and Taran.

Ellidyr is proud, selfish, and mean. He believes that honor is the glory you win from fighting a battle. His idea of honor is illustrated in this passage:

"We should make our stand now. Is this the honor we gain from following Gwydion? To let ourselves be tracked down like animals?"

Ellidyr follows his selfish search for glory until the very end of the novel when he finally changes. This quote provides evidence of the change:

"I stole the cauldron out of pride, not evil. I swear to you that I would not have used it."

This quote reveals that Ellidyr is not as selfish as he once was, and that his concept of honor has changed. Despite the fact that with the cauldron, he probably could have ruled the country, he wouldn't have used it. This change demonstrates real growth in Ellidyr. He gains real honor when he sacrifices his own life to destroy the cauldron.

Another character in the novel is Adaon, who is the exact opposite of Ellidyr. Adaon is calm, loving, and pure, and he has a sense of peace and wisdom about him that makes you like him. Adaon's concept of honor is that it doesn't matter how many battles you win. Honor is the feeling inside when you accept a challenge or beat yourself. The following quote explains his concept of honor:

"I have marched in many a battle host, but I have also planted seeds and reaped the harvest with my own hands. I have learned there is greater honor in a field well plowed than in a field steeped in blood."

This comment clearly shows that Adaon finds honor in living life fully and close to nature, not in killing or war. Another quote to support his idea is this:

"Is there not glory enough in living these days given to us? You should know there is adventure in simply being among the ones we love and things we love, and beauty, too."

This is Adaon's concept of honor, and it never changes. His bright outlook on life helps everyone around him.

The last major character in the novel is Taran, the hot-tempered protagonist who changes the most. At the beginning, Taran's view of honor is like Ellidyr's. Honor is won on the battlefield, not by working the earth. These words illustrate his concept:

"I am proud to serve Lord Gwydion, and there is a chance to win much honor, more than by washing pigs and weeding gardens."

**Response to Literature—Score 4 (continued)**

This quote reveals the similarities between Ellidyr's and Taran's beliefs about honor. Fortunately, Taran doesn't stay with Ellidyr's honor system. Later in the novel, as he changes, his ideas about honor change also. This quote reflects that change:

"It is Ellidyr who has paid the final price," Taran said slowly. "The last honor belongs to him."

In saying these words, Taran is admitting that Ellidyr paid a higher price than he did. At this point, Taran has grown into a man like Adaon, wise, honest, and forgiving. He has changed for the better, to everyone's benefit and become a true leader.

*The Black Cauldron* is an excellent book that teaches much about honor, growth, and overcoming challenges.

# Scoring Model for Response to Literature

## Score 3

This writer presents a clearly organized response to literature supported with details and specific examples.

**Strong Points:**

1. Satisfactory introduction and thesis statement
2. Logical organization
3. Some specific examples used to support main ideas

**Problem Points:**

1. Limited conclusions drawn from the evidence presented
2. Some unnecessary information
3. Abrupt ending; no conclusion
4. Some mechanical errors

### The Concept of Honor in *The Black Cauldron*

Lloyd Alexander's novel, *The Black Cauldron*, tells about a band of people going to and destroying the black cauldron to keep it out of the hands of Arawn who wanted to use it for evil purposes. It is about Ellidyr, Adaon, and Taran's concept of honor.

When Ellidyr, Prince of pen-Larcau, was first met "his hair was tawny, his eyes black and deep set in a pale, arrogant face." To Ellidyr, honor is about being the best and not letting other people tell you what to do. About half way through the book Taran tries to help Ellidyr's horse. Ellidyr keeps saying no. Finally he says yes. Taran sees there is a stone in his horse's shoe. He gets it out with a knife. Ellidyr says to Taran "you have tried to steal honor from me, pig-boy. Will you now rob me of my horse?" Taran replies "Your honor is your own and so is your steed. What stone is in your shoe, Prince of Pen-Larcau?" Ellidyr is always concerned about his honor. He is always trying to be the best.

Our next character, Adaon, has a totally different concept of honor. "Adaon, Taran saw, was tall, with straight black hair that fell to his shoulders." Adaon's concept of honor is that it does not matter about glory and pride. Adaon once said, "I have marched in many a battle host, but I have also planted seeds and reaped the harvest with my own hands. And I have learned there is greater honor in a field well plowed than in a field steeped in blood." This is saying it is better to give than to get. Adaon died later in the novel.

Our last character, Taran, is the main character in this novel. He says, "I am Taran, Assistant Pig-Keeper." Taran and Ellidyr keep competing to see who has more honor. In the beginning Taran and Ellidyr are racing. Ellidyr pushed Taran off a cliff. Taran got blamed for it. When Adaon dies, he gives Taran his brooch.

# Scoring Model for Response to Literature

## Score 2

While this writer presents a clear focus in this response to literature, the essay's weaknesses outweigh its strengths.

### Strong Point:

Clear focus and organization

### Problem Points:

1. Insufficient background information
2. Inadequate explanation and details to support main points
3. Lack of specific examples from the text
4. Vague evaluative terms
5. Awkward and faulty sentence structures
6. Numerous mechanical errors
7. Abrupt ending

## Honer in *The Black Cauldron*

Lloyd Alexander's book, *The Black Cauldron*, has danger, evil, and fantacy all brout together to make a wonderful book. This essay is about concepts of honer between three diferent peoples, Prince Ellidyr, Adaon, and Taran. Prince Ellidyr's concept of honer at the beginning of the novel was who could shed the most blood in battle. Later in the book he realized that not everything was about blood shed and battle and he gives up his honor of bringing the caldron back by hisself when he freed Taran and everyone by throwing hisself into the caldron and destroing it.

In addition to Prince Ellidyr Adaon was another character in this book. Adaon's concept of honer was not about blood shed or who won the most battles. He thout honer meant doing all of your work well. Adaon said, "My concept of honer is not a field steeped in blood but a field well plowed"

Also there was Taran, that was the assistant pig keeper of Caer Dallben. Taran was the main character of the book. At the beginning Taran's concept of honer was the same as Ellidyr but Taran changed later in the novel and relized that there was realy more honer in a field well plowed. At the end both Ellidyr and Taran learn the truth about honer.

# Scoring Model for Response to Literature

## Score 1

This writer's attempts to explore the concept of honor in *The Black Cauldron* are unsuccessful.

### Problem Points:

1.  No clear thesis statement
2.  Scattered, inconsistent focus
3.  Limited details
4.  Unclear how quotations support insights
5.  Few insights and conclusions
6.  Many mechanical errors

### The Black Cauldren

Loyd Alexender's novel *The Black Cauldren* explains about honor, The Black Cauldren, and the adventur of a pig keepers assistant named Taran. The Black cauldren is a pot that arawn an evil king uses to get warriors. When you put a dead body into the cauldren, the body's spiret becomes a warrior that cant killed. One of the characters is a impatiant man named Elidyer. Ellidyer beleves that honore is only for nights like him and not Taran. as Elidyer said "There is no honore in a pig boy!! Another character, totally oppisit of Ellidyer is a peacful man named Adaon. Adaon has a brooch wich allows him to be a leader Adaons concept of honore is everyone can share. "Many people deserve honore not just you." Taran is the star of the book. He starts out as a hot temperd man, but turns to be a leader. Taran thinks honore doesn't matter. Thie relates to both men by they all think honore is important. Taran at first thout about nothing but honore and growed up to be a leader. Taran and everyone change throuout the story in each way.

# Scoring Model for Exposition: Comparison-and-Contrast Essay

## Score 4

This writer presents a strong comparison-and-contrast essay with a consistent organizational strategy and effective elaboration.

## Strong Points:

1. Attracts reader's interest
2. Clear, consistent organization
3. Elaborates ideas with facts, details, and examples
4. Uses all information for comparison and contrast
5. Excellent command of grammar
6. Good sentence variety
7. Very few mechanical errors

### Meg and I Compared

Madeleine L'Engle's book *A Wrinkle in Time* is a tale of good vs. evil. The main characters, Meg, her brother Charles, Calvin, and Mr. Murry, join forces to fight against an evil force. Here I will compare the differences and similarities between Meg's personality and mine.

In some ways Meg and I are very similar. To start off, we both sometimes feel out of place at school. For example, I sometimes feel awkward because I'm a little shy at school and often think people are judging me. Similarly, Meg feels this emotion not only at school but at home, too. When she is at school, she feels stupid, ugly, and out of place. At home, she also feels bitterly out of place.

Furthermore, Meg and I have a second similarity in common; we both like to do things in our own way. One such way is that in math, I sometimes find another way to do the problems or ask my father to help me. Likewise, Meg is stubborn about the way she carries out things. When she comes home to do her homework, her father teaches her shortcuts to work the problems out. When she goes to school again, the other kids are working the problems differently, and this confuses Meg.

Finally, the third similarity between Meg and me is that we are both impatient. As an illustration, I was very impatient to put up the Christmas tree this year because the tree makes the house smell good. In the same way, Meg also wants to get things done quickly at times. She was impatient to find her father right away, but Charles and Calvin wanted to think things through first. In conclusion, Meg and I have an assortment of similarities in common.

Although Meg and I have many traits in common, there are other traits that are different. To begin with, I am pretty happy most of the time, but Meg gets depressed and feels sorry for herself. As proof, I don't let small things make me sad. When my little brother makes fun of me and calls me ugly, I just laugh him off. However, Meg takes people's words literally and spends a lot of time feeling sorry for herself. When kids at school tease her, she takes what they say to heart and believes that she is stupid. This is bad for her self-esteem.

In addition, the next difference is that we express our emotions differently. For instance, I am quieter and don't throw tantrums. When I get aggravated, I have a good cry and then feel a lot better. Meg, on the other hand, expresses her emotions loudly. She screams and yells, and gets into fights. When someone made fun of her brother, she beat up the kid. She never has bottled up emotions inside of her.

The third and final difference between Meg and me is that I sometimes struggle in math, but Meg is very advanced in it. I like math, but sometimes get confused. I know how to work out the equations, but I get frustrated. Unlike me, Meg is really good in math. She helped Calvin with his homework once, and he is several grades ahead of her. Meg can also make up her own shortcuts to figure out the problems. To summarize, Meg and I also have significant differences.

Altogether, *A Wrinkle in Time*, by Madeleine L'Engle is exciting and opens minds to new and different ideas. I have various similarities and differences with one of the book's main characters, Meg.

# Scoring Model for Exposition: Comparison-and-Contrast Essay

## Score 3

This writer presents a well-elaborated comparison-and-contrast essay with clear organization.

### Strong Points:

1.  Solid organization
2.  Elaborates most ideas with facts, details, or examples
3.  Engages audience interest
4.  Some transitions
5.  Adequate vocabulary and sentence construction

### Problem Points:

1.  Mechanical errors and insufficient punctuation
2.  Grammatical errors
3.  Occasional run-on sentences

### Comazotz and Earth

*A Wrinkle in Time* by Madeliene L'Engle is a very creative, wonderful science fiction story that involves travel across space and time. It is set here on Earth and also on a planet called Camazotz. The story concerns a family called the Murrys who embark on a journey to find their father. To find him they must travel to Camazotz, a distant planet, that is different from Earth yet similar too. The similarities and differences between the two are important to the story.

Camazotz and Earth have many similarites. To begin with, the people on these planets both feel emotions. For instance when Charles picks up a ball belonging to a child from Camazotz, the motherly figure is surprised and afraid and slams the door on him. Just as the mothers on Camazotz worry the fathers on earth worry about their children. When children go out to a party, dance, or the movies the parents worry about them. Some kids have gotten kidnapped. Therefore parents fear for their children's safety.

Another similarity between people on Camazotz and Earth are the employment opportunities. One certain job on Camazotz is to be a scientist. In the CENTRAL Central Intelligence Center, the people perform experiments, mostly on living creatures including humans. Similarly people on Earth also have the opportunity to be scientists. People do perform experiments on living creatures such as mice, rats, guinea pigs. Furthermore a third similarity between Camazotz and Earth is the vegetation. For example on Camazotz they have trees, grass, shrubs, and flowers, which would make Camazotz not as gloomy. In the same way Earth has trees, shrubs, and flowers, which make Earth less dark and gloomy. In conclusion the planets of Camazotz and Earth have many similarites.

Camazotz and Earth have quite a few similarites. But on the other hand they have many differences. To begin with on Camazotz everything is done in unison, Earth is not this way. For instance when the children were playing outside the balls were bounced and caught at the same time. The jump ropes hit the ground at the same time and doors opened in unison. Unlike Camazotz people on Earth don't do everything in unison, while one child is playing basketball another child could be playing hopscotch. There is not a rythm to everything on Earth as there is on Camazotz.

Another difference between Camaztoz and Earth is The Black Thing. Camazotz is completely controlled by The Black Thing that makes them do everything in unison, the people on Camazotz don't make decisions for themselves. They are convinced that being the same as everybody is safer and happier. However Earth is not controlled by The Black Thing. People on Earth make their own decisions and do what they want whenever they want.

Finally there is another difference between Camazotz and Earth which is in their technology levels. For example Camazotz has very advanced technology. Most people on Camazotz can rearrange the atoms in a wall to walk through it. They also have transparent columns that are as solid as a regular wall but these can be walked through with a certain power. This power requires advanced technology. Earth dosen't have technology that is as advanced as Camazotz. In summary Camazotz and Earth have many similarates yet many differences too.

In conclusion *A Wrinkle in Time* by Madeliene L'Engle is an exciting and imaginative book and part of it's excitement comes from way the characters travel to another world that is both strangely similar to our own planet and, at the same time wildly different.

# Scoring Model for Exposition: Comparison-and-Contrast Essay

## Score 2

While this writer has organized the ideas for this comparison-and-contrast essay, its weaknesses outweigh its strengths.

### Strong Points:

1. Provides reasons for comparison-and-contrast analysis
2. Fair organization
3. Moderate elaboration

### Problem Points:

1. Repetitive sentence structure
2. Lack of strong vocabulary
3. Digression from main points
4. Awkward sentence construction
5. Numerous mechanical errors

### Me Compared to Meg

*A Wrinkle in Time* by Madeleine L'Engle is a book about a girl named Meg and how she goes on a long and adventurus jurney to find her father who disappeared. This wunderful book by a great author. She leaves peoples hanging there for its hard to put the book down.

Meg and me both have similar and different personalities. Meg and me have similar personalities. Meg and me are both good in mathmatics Meg is so good at math that she helped Calvin with his high school work and she is only in the 7th grade. Likewize I do well on most math tests and I help others. Both of us are bitterly impatient Meg wanted to keep moving to find her father, but the others, were taking their sweet time. I am impatient when I go to different places. When I go to the grocery store with my mother, I bug her until we leave I always tell her you got 10 minutes left or 30 minutes left. Both of us are bitterly suspicious of strangers. Meg was suspicus of Mrs. Whatsit when she first saw her. I am suspicus of people who sell things door-todoor its almost like when I answer the door, I think there going to push me and rob me clean. Its easily recognizible that both of us have similar personalitys.

Meg and I have similar personalitys butalso have differences. Meg is very stubborn, but I am not. Meg is stubborn and she always has to be right she also doesn't take anything from anybody. When the boy was making fun of her brothers she beat up the boy. I am not stubborn because I don't care if things are perfect. Meg has low self esteem I have high self esteem due to certain reasons. Meg has low self esteem when kids at her school make fun of her I have high self esteem because I don't get picked on by kids. Meg shows emotions, but I don't like to show mine in front of other people. Meg cried about being picked on at school. I don't like to show my emotions in front of people. Thinking about things and possibly crying about them. meg and me have different personalitys.

# Scoring Model for Exposition: Comparison-and-Contrast Essay

## Score 1

This writer's efforts to write a comparison-and-contrast essay are unsuccessful.

### Problem Points

1. No reason provided for comparison-and-contrast analysis
2. Lack of organizational strategy
3. Inconsistent focus
4. Lack of facts or examples to support comparison and contrast
5. Uneven and confusing use of language
6. Many mechanical errors

### Meg and Marty

The story *A Wrinkle in Time by* Madeleine L'Engle about the strugles of the Murry family and how they go on a frantic serch for Megs father and find a way to save earth from an evil thing. This hart warming book that will tuch you harts and you wont never be able to put it down.

Meg and my friend Marty is very stuborn when it come to getting what they want. Marty is very stuborn when she don't get her way because her mom spoil her bad if Marty starts to cry her mom will get her any thing she wants. When I go to the store with Marty and her mom said she would get us a little something marty comes back with the hole basket full of things and her mom usually ends up buying me nothing and she buys her everything. Marty don't have no friends at school, and if Marty tryies to be friendley, she always ends up being mean because she can't controll her feelings like Meg has no friends because she doesn't trust anybody she thinks that they are probly going to make fun of her so therefor Meg can't trust anyone.

Marty and Meg also have many diferences to. The first diference they have is that marty is a style freek and always into style even though she never talks about it her real personalty is very stylish she is into the new fashions in the world she wants to be a super modle and a chloths designer. She is always wanting to go shopping and by some clothes. Meg doesn't tho she never realy got to change her clothes. In cunclusion, this book by Madeleine L'Engle shows how they all go on a frantic serch for Megs and Charles father.

# Scoring Model for Exposition: Cause-and-Effect Essay

## Score 4

This writer presents a well-organized cause-and-effect essay with elaboration, effective vocabulary, and a clear writing style.

## Strong Points:

1. Clearly stated purpose
2. Consistent organizational strategy
3. Full elaboration
4. Appropriate word choices
5. Clear transitions
6. Consistently linked causes and effects
7. Very few mechanical errors
8. Effective conclusion

## The Emancipation Proclamation: Lincoln Under Stress

"If my name ever goes into history, it will be for this act."
—Abraham Lincoln

Abraham Lincoln's understanding of the huge stakes involved in the Emancipation Proclamation caused him to make the statement above. The effect of the Emancipation Proclamation was a major change in the ways of a great nation.

From reading *Lincoln, A Photobiography* by Russell Freedman, we see that there were many causes for the Emancipation Proclamation and that it had important results. However, it was one of the many tough decision Lincoln had to make alone because his generals would not make them during the American Civil War. At first, Lincoln wanted to ignore slavery because it was so controversial. Lincoln just wanted to keep the states as one united nation. He was afraid that freeing slaves would cause southerners to start their own nation. Since people called abolitionists put pressure on Lincoln, as well as the whole nation, to free slaves, Lincoln was afraid he would lose many northern supporters of the Civil War if he didn't do something about slavery. So he came up with the idea of paying southerners the price of their slaves if they would set them free and stay in the union. He also knew this would cause many ex-slaves to join the Union Army. It badly needed able-bodied men because the North was losing the war against the secessionist states.

President Lincoln really opposed slavery himself, but he feared releasing slaves because the border states like Kentucky and Missouri were on the Union side and still had slaves. He hoped that emancipation would begin in the border states and spread south as states were conquered. Then the slaves could be re-settled in Africa or Central America. He was afraid that freeing all slaves would cause those border states to turn to the cause of the South to get their slaves back.

The effect of this plan was a large protest from the border state congressmen. These states needed slaves to run their plantations and they would not change their way of life.

Lincoln still wanted to do the right thing, but he wasn't sure the president even had the authority to free slaves. Some senators advised him he could because it was wartime and the union was in danger. Freeing slaves would weaken the South so it would be a war strategy. He would be acting as commander-in-chief of the army. Therefore, Lincoln was convinced to proclaime the end of slavery in all states that did not come back into the union by a certain date. This would make the border states happy, and he would work for emancipation later in a way fair to those states that returned.

One problem was that the North was still losing the war and ending slavery would look like an act of desperation. So he waited until the North won a significant battle at Antietam. When he issued the proclamation in September, 1862, it caused all Black people and abolitionists to rejoice. Another result was that several Union Army Black regiments were quickly formed.

The war was causing Lincoln much stress. He was tired and his hand shook as he signed the Emancipation Proclamation with a gold pen. But this act of bravery by the weary president had the effect of freeing millions of men, women, and children from slavery, and Lincoln became a hero.

# Scoring Model for Exposition: Cause-and-Effect Essay

## Score 3

This writer presents a well-organized cause-and-effect essay with some elaboration and appropriate examples.

### Strong Points:

1. Clearly stated purpose
2. Sequential organization linking causes and effects
3. Elaborated cause-and-effect relationships
4. Few mechanical errors

### Problem Points:

1. Insufficient explanation of some examples
2. Vague references
3. Verb tense inconsistency
4. Some spelling errors
5. Some run-on sentences

## Lincoln Frees the Slaves

Abraham Lincoln had a hard time deciding what to do about slavery at the time of the Civil War in America. He knew down deep that he wanted everyone to be free and so he wrote the Emancipation Proclamation. There are many causes for his writing the Emancipation Proclamation, and there were many effects from it.

One cause was Lincoln's personal opposition to slavery. Therefore, it was nearly a sure thing that the Emancipation Proclamation would come about some day. Another cause was that the North needed soldiers in the army. Freeing slaves would supply many many soldiers for armies. Also some people believed that human freedom is as important as a united nation. A large number of people believed the freedom of the southern slaves was important just because they all believed in freedom itself.

These diversities in belief about freedom and slavery were one of the causes that led Lincoln to say he opposed slavery when the Civil War began. This lead to his popularity in the North during the war. It also had the effect of leading to Lincoln's assasination by a Confederate slavery believer. This was an extremely sad event.

Early in the war Lincoln had a plan for a proclamation to abolish slavery which he discussed with some of his friends and some of them agreed to the plan while some did not. He listened to one of his cabinet secretaries who said he should not carry out his plan because it would look like an act of desparation. At that time the North was losing the war and the secretary told Lincoln he should try later if the North is winning.

Although Lincoln was an open minded man who was not afraid to say what he thought he did wait until the Union Army won a big battle As a result of the victory, he signed the Emancipation Proclamation with a gold pen in an impressive ceremony.

These were all causes for the Emancipation Proclamation which freed the slaves and ended a war. We learn from the past and change the future. The effects of the proclamation are still felt today. The South had lost people to pick cotten and the way of life would change alot from the days of the big plantations. The slaves were free and would begin making their way up in the world in education and economics. Lincoln himself would be long honored for the part he played in the freedom of slaves even to the present day. All these are important effects of his signing of the Emancipation Proclamation.

# Scoring Model for Exposition: Cause-and-Effect Essay

## Score 2

Although this writer has organized causes and elaborated effects, this cause-and-effect essay's weaknesses outweigh its strengths.

### Strong Points:

1. Some organization
2. Some attempt at cause-and-effect reasoning
3. Some elaboration of details

### Problem Points:

1. Lacks statement of purpose
2. Illogical progression of main points; unclear exposition
3. Missing transitions
4. Extraneous material
5. Many mechanical errors

## Lincoln Gets His Wish

When Lincoln signed the Emancipation Proclamation, one effect Lincoln had was to get his wish—slavery demolished. One cause was abolitionists telling Lincoln he had to do it.

I learned more about slaves. People bought slaves so they could have huge farms and have peoples to do all thee work to raze crops. The white people who ownd slaves got rich and powerful while the slaves had no money or name and when slaves had babies the owners got free workers. Slaves werent educated be cus they not alowed to learn or read or anything.

One cause of the Civil War was that Lincoln didn't want the south to be there own country. The north need more troops so they need to free the slaves. Human freedom is exactly what we fought for when we fought the british. Just like the Civil war.

A main cause was that Lincoln opposed slavery. He knowed it was wrong and there shouldn't be slavery so he did something, he thought it was not fare that people were treated different.

Before Lincoln died in assasintion, he wrote the Emancipation proclamation. Lincoln sined the proclamation and all slaves were freed. Some joined the norths army and gave up their lives for the country. Lincoln is also gave up his life while serving the country as a great president who helped all people have freedom.

# Scoring Model for Exposition: Cause-and-Effect Essay

## Score 1

This writer's efforts to write an effective cause-and-effect essay are unsuccessful.

### Problem Points:

1. Introduction lacks cause-and-effect thesis statement
2. Unclear organization
3. Unclear cause-and-effect relationships
4. Lack of elaboration
5. Vague and confusing pronoun references
6. Grammatical and mechanical errors
7. Poor relation of conclusion to main points

## Ending Slavery

Russell Freedman wrote a story about A. Lincoln and made it into a book with many pictures called "Lincoln: A Photobiography." I write about how A. Lincoln freed slavery. The reason he want to them becuse the union army need peoples to fight the south. Slaves could join the army but the south want to keep slaves to work.

The Civil War was started by Lincoln to keep the states in the contry and over slavery then he changed his mind and some men got after him to free slaves and make the emancipation proclamation. The south react to this and they beome the Confedrate States. The Confedrate and the union the got back together because since they were so worked up about a limited nation, human freedom had equal importence

This war hapened a long time ago. In the end the north side won the war on Lincolns side. So there wasnt no slavery. And then Lincoln died with a note that went a little like this If my name go down in history, it shall be for this." Something like that. And then he sadly died.

# Scoring Model for Exposition: Explanation of a Process

## Score 4

This paper is a clear, well-organized process explanation.

## Strong Points:

1. Clear focus on procedures leading to a well-defined end
2. Rules presented in logical order
3. Complicated actions described in adequate detail
4. Overall clarity and fluency
5. Mature choice of vocabulary
6. Effective transitions
7. Few mechanical errors

### Learn How to Play Twister

Everyone has a favorite game. Sometimes it can be confusing to learn to play a new game. Twister is a very simple but fun game to play. All you need are the mat, the spinner, and two or more people.

First, the most important parts to the game are the mat and the spinner. The mat is a large plastic square about the size of a bed sheet. It is covered with large, multicolored dots about the size of a foot or a hand. The spinner is a board with the colors of the dots from the mat and the words, "right foot," "left foot," "right hand," and "left hand" repeated beside different colors. The spinner lands on a different color with every turn.

The rules state that first a player spins the spinner. Whichever hand or foot the spinner points to on the board the player must place on the mat, on a dot of the same color. Next, another player spins the spinner and places his left or right hand or foot on a dot of the matching color. The players take turns spinning and placing their hands and feet on the dots on the mat.

The game moves along quickly, with the difficulty increasing as more players are added. You can imagine how crazy the game can get as each player spins and has to move hands and feet to different colored dots. Although the game can be played with two to five people, it gets crazier with each added player.

Players continue playing until one by one they fall or put their hands or feet in the wrong space. Sometimes a player is unable to maneuver to place his or her hand or foot on the right colored dot. When this happens, the player is out of the game. Also, if a player loses balance and falls down, he or she is out of the game. The game continues until there is only one player left; that player is declared the winner!

As stated earlier, the minimum number of players is two, the maximum is five. Any more than five and it gets too crowded, causing people to tumble on top of each other. The optimum number of players is four.

Twister is one of my favorite games. After hearing how it's played, I hope you agree to join me in a game very soon. I am sure you will find it an enjoyable way to have a good time with friends.

# Scoring Model for Exposition: Explanation of a Process

## Score 3

This paper presents an organized process explanation with clear step-by-step procedures.

## Strong Points:

1. Focus on procedures explaining the game
2. Instructions presented in logical order
3. Some use of elaboration
4. Some transitions

## Problem Points:

1. Step-by-step procedure breaks down and becomes unclear
2. Some missing information
3. A few errors of usage

### Learn How to Play Hopscotch

There are lots of fun and interesting games to play. Hopscotch is one of my favorite childhood games to play. Playing hopscotch is simple and easy, that's why I like it so much. I will tell you exactly how to play it.

First the game has to be played on a hard surface, like concrete or cement. A courtyard or flat driveway will do nicely just as long as it's flat and smooth. The game has ten equal sized squares numbered 1–10. The squares are drawn on the flat surface with chalk. The squares are placed first 1 and 2, side by side, next 3, then 4 and 5, side by side, then 6, 7, and 8, one above the other. Last 9 and 10 are drawn side by side above 8.

The only material you need to play is a beanbag. You throw the beanbag onto any square you want then hop to it. You hop on one or both feet depending on which square you land upon. After hopping over the beanbag, you bend over to pick it up then hop back to the beginning.

There are several versions of the game. Some people play that you must throw the beanbag on to the numbered squares in order, beginning with square 1. Some people play that you may throw the beanbag on to any square you wish. The object of the game is to pick up the beanbag from every square without falling.

Hopscotch is an easy, but fun game to play. I always loved playing it and I'm sure that you will too!

# Scoring Model for Exposition: Explanation of a Process

## Score 2

Although this writer has attempted to write an effective process explanation the explanation's weaknesses outweigh its strengths.

### Strong Points:

1. Logical sequence of procedures

### Problem Points:

1. Vague explanations of procedures
2. Some confusing details
3. Weak elaboration
4. No variety in sentence structure
5. Many mechanical errors

## Learn to Play Don't Break the Ice

I just got off the phone with my friend. I called to invite her over to play a fun and exciting game of Don't Break the Ice. The only problim is she sid she's never played it befor. That means I'm goining to have to explain it to her.

First you have to set up the stand looks like a stool with a squar hole in the middle. You turn it upside down and put little squar pieces in the senter until they are very tite, then you flip it over the peaces should stay in place.

You put a plastic man on the senter cube. In the box there is 2 plastic hamer-type things. You take the hamers out of the box and one to each person, your now ready to hit the cubes.

Last, you break the ice! One person at a time take there hamer and gets one wack at a cube. The object is to NOT knock down the man in the middle. Whoever does, loses. Now that you know to play Don't Break the Ice, go out and play it, I only hope my friend will catch on as quikly as you do.

# Scoring Model for Exposition: Explanation of a Process

## Score 1

This writer's process explanation is unsuccessful.

## Problem Points:

1. Missing necessary information
2. Incomplete thoughts and steps
3. Unclear and disorganized instructions
4. Insufficient details; no elaboration
5. Many distracting and confusing mechanical errors
6. Sentence fragments; missing words
7. No conclusion

### Play Tunk

I'm going teach you about to play Tunk. Tunk is a cool wants you learn how to play. There is certain things like the rules, card, etc, the rules because without the rules you want know what to do. The first rule is that you get any odd number and if you pick up a card and put it down the othe person can pick it up but if they don't that card is dead. If you lay your card down that means you drop.

Tunk is about having matches like 3456 of harts. You have to have a least three of the same sut. You have 3, twos or any number.

# Scoring Model for Writing for Assessment

## Score 4

This writer presents a well-elaborated persuasive essay for assessment with a clear, consistent organizational strategy and effective word choice.

## Strong Points:

1. Clearly defined thesis statement
2. Supporting details appropriate to the specific audience
3. Clear, consistent, and logical organization
4. Fully elaborated points that support the thesis
5. Effective transitions between ideas
6. Highly effective word choices
7. Excellent sentence variety
8. Few mechanical errors

### Video Games in the Cafeteria

It has come to my attention that the addition of video games to the cafeteria is being considered. I am against this proposal entirely and wish to share some of the reasons for my concerns.

First of all, the addition of video games to our cafeteria would result in a more chaotic lunchroom than we have at present. Students would gather around the machines yelling, cheering, and probably arguing about the game. When students hear cheering, booing, etc., they want to know what is going on and often stand up or yell across the cafeteria to see what all the ruckus is about. (This does not happen very often at the present time, but I am sure it would occur more frequently after the addition of video games.) Other students, who simply want to eat and speak to their friends, would have to talk over all the other noise. This would be unbearable for the students and teachers in the cafeteria and it might even disturb nearby classes. I know that by now you are well aware of the trivial things students fight over. If video games were added to our lunch room, there would be further fights over such issues as whose turn it is, who is the best at what game, which game is better, and many other petty arguments.

This proposed change in the cafeteria would negatively affect the rest of the day for any student who participated in these games. For example, students would prefer playing games to eating. They would be playing games, and/or standing in line waiting to play games, or dawdling near the games instead of eating. Students our age are most likely to be hungry, irritable, and tired by fifth period because of lack of nutrition. Because of this, they may not be able to work as well or may miss out on important instructions, which would ultimately affect their grade.

Furthermore, adding video games to the cafeteria would give the principals extra work and would most likely cause them additional stress. They would have the job of making a whole new list of cafeteria rules explaining times, ways and turns to play the games. Therefore, they would have to add more teachers to the cafeteria in order to enforce these laws.

Still another concern is that video games are expensive. Our students would have to have additional fund-raisers in order to buy these games, which do not in any way contribute to their education. This would be a wasteful use of the money that could be spent on computers, software, and especially new textbooks. All of these are much more important than any arcade game.

In conclusion, please reconsider the addition of video games to our school cafeteria. I am convinced that the addition would not be at all good for our school and would be more trouble than it is worth.

# Scoring Model for Writing for Assessment

## Score 3

This writer presents a persuasive essay for assessment, using a clear organizational strategy and effective support.

### Strong Points:

1. Clearly identified thesis
2. Clear organizational strategy with some inconsistencies
3. Connected ideas
4. Adequate sentence variety and vocabulary
5. Details to support thesis

### Problem Points:

1. Insufficient elaboration
2. Some problems with sentence structure
3. Some mechanical errors

## Video Games in the Cafeteria

I think it would be a bad idea to put video games in the cafeteria. Here are some reasons why not to put video/arcade games in the cafeteria.

First, it's likely that students would skip classes and go to the cafeteria to play video games. They might forget about the time, which would cause them to miss other classes. As a result they would not know what was going on in classes and would get behind. They might even end up flunking the 7th or 8th grade.

Secondly, the students might start to fight over the video games. Students eating in the cafeteria could be bothered by the noise and fighting. When they fight some students could end up getting hurt or hurting others. This could lead to some students getting put in alternative schools. Also food fights might start to happen. And students would get hurt then to.

Finally, people would start to break the machines. The video games would already be paid for by the taxpayers. However, they would have to be fixed by the taxpayers or the school. Some of these machines get pretty expensive. The video games also cost a lot of money.

In conclusion, I am convinced, and hope that you are also, that video games should not be put in the cafeteria.

# Scoring Model for Writing for Assessment

## Score 2

This writer presents an organized persuasive essay for assessment, but its weaknesses outweigh its strengths.

### Strong Points:

1. Organizational strategy
2. Thesis statement

### Problem Points

1. Some inappropriate word choices and details
2. No clear transitions
3. Insufficient elaboration
4. Repetitive vocabulary
5. No sentence variety
6. Numerous mechanical errors

### Video Games

I'm against video games in the cafateria because they makes to much trouble.

Video games will start a fight because the big kids on the game will not take turns and make the little kids feel bad. Some of the kids will skip in line and that will cause a fight. video games will cause some kids to skip class and that will cause a big affect on them for instance. If they skip they will not pass some of there classes. Playing the game to long, and staying in line to long because you went your turn.

Video games will cause kids to break the machine. For example the kids can break the machine. The machine will take the kids mony and then they will get mad, they will get mad at the game because they can not bet the game.

I know you have spent a lot of money on the machine in the cafateria. But I think its not good to put a game in the cafateria.

# Scoring Model for Writing for Assessment

## Score 1

This writer's attempt to present a persuasive essay for assessment is unsuccessful.

### Problem Points:

1. No position statement
2. Lack of organizational strategy
3. Inappropriate word choices and details
4. Lack of elaboration
5. Confusing, poor use of language
6. Many grammar, spelling, and punctuation errors

### Video Games

In many school districts, video games has been causeing bad things to hap-ping, I think this issue is important because it has affect this school. For ex-ample, skipping class an going to the cafteria to play the game. Telling teachers that you have to go to the bathroom but you don't. When its lunch time you stay in the lunch room. Or being late to class all the time and no pa-nalty an class.

It cheat you money on the video game, like getting the game to start or the game will say you have 3 games but you only got one. To much fighting will get you trouble, if you were playing the game the person back of you will get made at the person an started to push him. Well, I realy think this is a bad idea to put video game in the cafteria.

# Materials for Parent Interaction

# To the Teacher

Successful secondary education relies on continued open interaction with students and their parents. While you are the primary instructor, encouraging parents or guardians to take an active interest in their child's education in the following ways can help to reinforce the work that you do in the classroom:

- *Showing interest in a student's work and progress:* The interested parent validates the importance of school instruction, activities, and tests. Parents who provide support for students may also reinforce good study habits and encourage students to organize their time and get assignments done. In contrast, students whose parents are disinterested in their school work may learn to be disinterested as well.

- *Monitoring homework:* Parents who monitor homework can help students stay on task and keep up with the learning that has been introduced in class. In addition, parents are the first line of help. Parents who work with their children can help identify problem areas and deficiencies and encourage the student to seek further help. If a lesson or concept seems problematic, a parent could contact you to make appropriate plans.

- *Extending and/or enriching instruction:* When parents are aware of the specific content and concepts a child is learning, they are more likely to help the student make community connections or real-world applications. For example, when a student is learning to analyze media, a parent might initiate discussions about the television the family watches at home. Alternatively, when a student is learning about the Vietnam War or subsequent historic events, the parent might encourage the child to talk with relatives about their personal experiences or thoughts about the event.

As a teacher, you should take steps to build a good relationship with the parents and guardians of your students, such as the following:

- Sharing your state standards.

- Explaining the district's curriculum and assessment program.

- Encouraging parents to review the textbook.

- Providing timely, informative feedback about each student's assignments and progress.

The pages that follow offer you specific forms to establish and support the home-school connection.

# Parent Welcome

Date: _____

Dear Parent or Guardian:

Recent studies show how important parental involvement is in helping students to achieve success in school. Because I know that you want your child to have an excellent year in English, I'm pleased to tell you about our curriculum and suggest some ways you can participate in improving your child's performance.

Our English textbook this year will be *Prentice Hall Literature: Timeless Voices, Timeless Themes.* This program combines a wide variety of quality reading selections with literature analysis, critical thinking and reading skills, and composition. Importantly, it connects the literature to students' own experiences through the development of themes relevant to students' lives.

You can help your child get the most from this program and from all of his or her homework by following this expert-tested advice:

- **Find the best time for studying.** Work with your teenager to decide on the best time for studying. Then, set that time aside at least five days out of every week. If there is no homework, your child can use the time to review or plan ahead.
- **Eliminate common distractions.** Set aside a study area that is free from noise and other distractions. Turn off the TV. Your teenager may say that watching television is helpful, but no research supports this. In fact, watching television allows students to "turn off their minds" because it requires no action or interaction.
- **Avoid common interruptions.** Take messages if the telephone rings, and have your teenager alert his or her friends not to drop by during the established study time.
- **Provide physical conditions that help concentration.** Ensure that the study area has adequate lighting and is kept at a comfortable temperature. Provide a table or desk that has enough space for writing.
- **Keep supplies handy.** Keeping study materials nearby saves time. Placing them in a small bucket or box makes it easy to move them to the study area.
- **Encourage computer literacy.** Help your teenager to see the value of using the computer to write compositions and other assignments. Encourage your child to use the computers at home, school, or the public library.
- **Ask to see your child's books.** Looking through the books gives you a better idea of what your teenager is learning and shows him or her that you think the material is important.
- **Ask to see your child's work on a regular basis.** You do not need to criticize or regrade the papers—that will only make your teenager less willing to show you his or her work. Just let your child know you are interested.
- **Read.** By watching you read, your teenager will see reading as a valuable activity. You can be especially effective if you occasionally read and discuss one of the selections your child is covering in class.

I look forward to working with your child and hope you will contact me if you have any questions during the school year.

Cordially,

_____

English Teacher

# Parent Letter:
# Review of State Standards

Date: _____

Dear Parent or Guardian:

   The state of _____ has established a set of English/Language Arts standards to ensure that all students in the state develop grade-level appropriate proficiencies in the Language Arts each year. I have attached the state standards to this sheet for your review. Please read, sign, and return this form. Feel free to indicate any questions or concerns you have. I will work to address any concerns you have about the instructional goals for this academic year.

                                            Cordially,

_____
English Teacher

_____

   I, the parent or guardian of _____, have reviewed the state standards in English/Language Arts for this academic year. I understand that these standards form the foundation for the instruction and educational expectations in the classroom.

_____
Parent

   Please use these lines to indicate any questions, concerns, or comments you would like the teacher to address:

_____

_____

_____

_____

_____

             

# Parent Letter:
# Selection Objectives and Standards Correlation

Date: _____

Dear Parent or Guardian:

In class, we are about to begin reading the following selection:

_____

The chart below indicates the selection objectives students will address, as well as the state standards that each objective develops.

| Domain | Skill or Strategy | Standards Correlation |
|---|---|---|
| Reading | | |
| Writing | | |
| Written and Oral English Language Conventions | | |
| Listening and Speaking | | |

These skills and strategies are intended to ensure your child's development in Language Arts. Please feel free to contact me if you have any questions.

Cordially,

_____

English Teacher

# Parent Letter: Writing Home Review

Name _____ Date _____

**To the Student:** Fill in the name of a family member or an adult friend, and attach this letter to the final version of your work to request comments on your work.

Date _____

Dear _____,

    I am attaching something that I wrote in school recently. I would appreciate it if you would read it and tell me what you think of it. I am particularly interested in getting your answers to the questions below. You can answer them on the lines under each question.

What do you think my purpose is for writing this?

_____

Were you able to follow my thoughts? If not, where did you get lost? What could I have done to make it easier to follow along?

_____

Is there any information that you wish I had included? If so, what?

_____

_____

Are there any parts that you think I could have left out? If so, which parts?

_____

_____

What do you like best about what I have written?

_____

_____

What else would you like to tell me about what I have written?

_____

_____

    Thank you for your help.

Sincerely yours,

_____

Writing Student

# Parent Letter:
# Portfolio Home Review

Date _____

Dear _____,

    I am attaching a portfolio of work that I completed in school recently. I would appreciate it if you would review the contents and tell me what you think of my work. You can do this by answering the questions below. To help you, I have filled in the first few lines so you will know the purpose of this portfolio.

    I value your opinion very much. By sharing your response to my work with me, you will help me to learn and to make improvements in my next portfolio.

The purpose of this portfolio is to show _____

_____.

Which item or items in the portfolio best support my purpose? What is it about them that strongly supports my purpose? _____

_____

Do any items in the portfolio seem weak or irrelevant? If so, which ones? What might I have done to strengthen them? _____

_____

Are there other things I might have included in my portfolio? How would they have helped? _____

_____

What else can you tell me about my portfolio? What suggestions would you offer for my next portfolio? _____

_____

    Thank you for your help.

Sincerely yours,

_____
Writing Student

**To the Teacher:** Have students attach this letter to their completed portfolios and use it to request comments on their portfolio from someone in the home.

# Homework Log

**Directions to the Student:** Use this form to record your homework assignments in Language Arts each day. When you have finished each assignment, place a check in the *Completed* column. Ask your parent or guardian to sign the form at the end of each week.

| Date | Assignment | Completed |
|------|-----------|-----------|
|      |           |           |
|      |           |           |
|      |           |           |
|      |           |           |
|      |           |           |
|      |           |           |
|      |           |           |
|      |           |           |
|      |           |           |
|      |           |           |

**Signature of Parent or Guardian** _____